THE WORLD'S BEST
SUPERFOODS
HEALTH-BOOSTING
RECIPES FROM
AROUND THE WORLD

MATT MUNRO © LONELY PLANET

CONTENTS

FOREWORD

BY NATASHA CORRETT OF HONESTLY HEALTHY

Growing up with a father ensconced in the restaurant industry, a mother highly allergic to wheat, gluten and dairy, and a godmother who is a nutritional therapist, it shouldn't come as a surprise that I became a chef focused on health. When I founded Honestly Healthy in 2010 my goal was to bring the knowledge I'd gained to the public, and help them improve their lives through the medium of food.

As much as I love creating healthy dishes out of nothing, I thoroughly enjoy playing with classic recipes with optimum health in mind. My Middle Eastern potato salad recipe (p136) is just such an example, taking the traditional potato salad and turning it on its head, with the addition of some superfoods (sweet potato and pomegranate), along with yoghurt, cinnamon and cumin. The addition of the spices was inspired by the aromas of dishes encountered while travelling – I love the herbs and spices in Middle Eastern food, and enjoy recreating

those flavours. Travelling can transform your cooking, exposing you to a new world of cuisine, whether it be different flavours, ingredients, dishes or even cooking methods. Travel can also introduce you to lasting loves – I'm now obsessed with tahini (p30).

As I'm always focused on health, superfoods – natural, nutrient-rich ingredients that are considered to be advantageous for people's health and well-being – tend to creep into my cooking (and daily diet) often. Each superfood has its own health properties, some of which have been celebrated for millennia – goji berries (p80) have been used in Chinese medicine for over 6000 years and are said to be the elixir of long life.

One superfood I particularly love to cook with is raw cacao (p16), perhaps because I have a seriously sweet tooth. This is chocolate in its natural state. It is incredibly bitter, but by just adding an unrefined syrup and some coconut oil you can make the simplest, most delicious raw chocolate. Packed full of nutritious antioxidants, it also gives you a natural energy kick – it's what I tend to reach for during an afternoon slump.

There are some superfoods that you'll now find all over the world in local markets: blueberries (p81), avocados (p82), turmeric... To get the most out of your superfoods, try eating them in a raw state – throw berries into a morning muesli (p68), mash up avocado on some toast (p112) or simply put some slices of fresh turmeric root in hot water with lemon in the morning to give you the kick that perhaps coffee once provided.

Eating healthily shouldn't just be about us, either – it should be about protecting our planet too, by reducing food wastage, and choosing sustainably produced ingredients that don't negatively impact the environment.

So with that in mind, get out there and discover for yourself the power of the superfood. Happy eating!

JUSTIN FOULKES, MATT MUNRO © LONELY PLANET

MATT MUNRO © LONELY PLANET

SYMBOLS

The superfoods in each recipe have been highlighted in the ingredients list. The potential health benefits that have been associated with these superfoods are noted with the following icons at the top of each entry.

 ENERGY

 IMMUNE SYSTEM

 DIGESTION

 LONGEVITY

 HEART

JUSTIN FOULKES ©LONELY PLANET

NIKADA © GETTY IMAGES

SEEDS & NUTS

Once disparaged as 'bird food', seeds and nuts are an important and oh-so-easy way to incorporate a mega vitamin and mineral explosion into your daily diet. Sprinkle on your cereal, bake in a handy-sized bar, crush into a paste, blend into a smoothie or – the most efficient method of all – pack an emergency handful of your favourite raw combination to snack on at work or in the car. Your body will thank you for it. →

HISTORY

Nuts and seeds have been an important energy source throughout history, and there are many references to them in ancient literature: almonds and pistachios are mentioned in writings from biblical times, and we know that Romans gave sugared almonds as gifts at weddings. In addition scientists believe that first humans ate nuts, in particular thanks to the results obtained from the analysis of tooth-enamel thickness and tooth microstructure of a hominid that lived in Africa 4.2 million years ago.

HEALTH BENEFITS

Studies have shown that in countries where people eat more nuts, the incidence of cardiovascular disease is generally lower. Previously avoided for a while because of their fat content, nuts and seeds have now been embraced as an important part of our daily diet. Apart from healthy fats, they supply carbohydrates, fibre, protein, and a variety of vitamins and essential nutrients. Just a handful of nuts can address the lack of minerals – magnesium, zinc, selenium and copper – in traditional Western diets. They also provide a degree of satiety, which in turn can help regulate weight.

GRANT FARIN © GETTY IMAGES, JUSTIN FOULKES © LONELY PLANET

VARIANTS

Along with raw nuts and seeds in your local health-food store, you may also notice nut and seed butters doing a roaring trade. Don't let the word 'butter' fool you: there's usually nothing of the kind in such spreads, just raw nuts blended into a paste. Peanut and almond butters seem to be the most popular, not to mention tahini (p30) – a well-known sesame-seed butter – but any nut or seed can be made into a butter or a spread. So long as your butter doesn't contain any preservatives or sweeteners, and is made from high-quality nuts or seeds, you'll be reaping similar benefits to eating the raw goods.

DID YOU KNOW?

Were you aware that a pistachio is a fruit? And a peanut is actually a legume? Not many people are! We've kept them in this section for ease of reference. Peanuts are often associated with 'nut' allergies, but studies have shown that mothers who ate peanuts during pregnancy had babies who were less likely to develop nut allergies in later life.

SEEDS

While nuts have always had their moment of glory, forming part of the Food Guide Pyramid put together by the US Department of Agriculture in 1992 (the Swedes published the first type of food pyramid in 1974), seeds were nowhere to be seen. It's fair to say they're making up for lost time and having quite a 'moment' in the superfoods world. This is because seeds have the holy trinity of healthy fats, fibre and protein. Just beware of all the modern hype that accompanies them. No single seed is a miracle weight-loss or cancer cure, but sprinkling them into your meals on a regular basis can only help not harm your health.

CHIA SEEDS

Pronounced 'chee-ah', these ancient seeds are ubiquitous at health-food shops. A tablespoon of chia seeds has more calcium than a glass of milk (ideal for the dairy intolerant), loads of Omega 3 fatty acids, which help the heart and brain function, as well as fibre for digestion and antioxidants for disease prevention.

CACAO

Ah, cacao: the raw chocolate wonder of the world. Containing 40 times the antioxidants of blueberries (p81) and more calcium than cow's milk, cacao is the highest plant-based source of iron. And, like, cocoa powder (which is raw cacao roasted at high temperatures), it also makes you feel good. What's not to like!

WATTLESEEDS

Part of the diet of indigenous Australians for over 40,000 years, wattleseeds have rapidly found fame as a native food rich in protein. They are dried and roasted like coffee and then ground into a powder, and mostly used as an ingredient in baking. Very helpful for diabetics, given the low glycemic levels.

STOCKCAM, 4KODIAK © GETTY IMAGES, ASHLEY MACKEVICIUS © STOCKFOOD

CHIA FOR YOUR PETS

The world is going so crazy for chia seeds: you can even find them in dog food these days, supposedly as a constipation aid, but also because the fatty acids can help in achieving a shiny coat. Cats with nervous stomachs or digestive problems can also benefit! Because chia can hold a vast amount of liquid, it acts as a soothing coating for the intestines and the lining of the stomach.

SESAME SEEDS

These tiny seeds are incredibly tasty toasted, and high in zinc: great for the immune system. They also contain more than a third of our copper intake, which is needed for energy and collagen production, not to mention manganese for bone health. In addition, they also help reduce blood pressure and assist in fighting inflammation in the body.

SCIENCE PHOTO LIBRARY; NIGEL PAVITT © GETTY IMAGES

NUTS

Forget your salted, greasy peanuts on a beer-soaked bar mat. And bypass those vendors selling sugar-coated, reheated excuses for nuts in tourist hotspots. For maximum nutritional benefit, we're only interested in the raw materials that nature provided here. Apart from a relatively recent development, that is, which is the pre-soaking or 'activating' of nuts. This has been done by indigenous cultures for years, and aids in digestion by reducing the amount of starch and fibre while enhancing protein and vitamin content.

WALNUTS
Of all the nuts, the walnut is king: it contains the highest levels of antioxidants, not to mention protein, abundant Vitamin E, and many other vitamins and minerals. Just don't roast walnuts; this reduces their antioxidant power.

ALMONDS
Excellent for lowering cholesterol, almonds have more fibre and calcium than most other nuts. You can also eat more of them, as they're relative low in calories and are a great source of Vitamin E, manganese and magnesium.

PISTACHIOS
Fun to crack open for their jewel-green appearance, pistachios are incredibly high in antioxidants, notably lutein, also found in leafy greens (see p118). A handful of pistachios has more potassium (and is certainly prettier) than a banana.

WALNUTS AND SYMBOLISM

Walnuts are seen as a potent symbol of masculinity. No, we can't think why either. But if you crack open one of these spherical beauties to observe the brain-shaped nut kernel inside, you'll understand why they also symbolise intellectual productivity. In Indian culture, dreaming of a breaking a walnut and finding it tasty is a good omen – regardless of your gender.

CASHEWS

Pretty close to being everyone's favourite nut, raw cashews are high in iron and soluble dietary fibre, and contain more folate and Vitamin K than other nuts. This is good news for your bones and for healthy blood clotting.

MACADAMIAS

The buttery flavour of macadamias can be addictive: this is the fat you're tasting! It's mostly of the monosaturated kind, which is good for your heart. These nuts are also a good source of thiamine, which is beneficial for the nervous system.

BRAZIL NUTS

Although high in Vitamin E, Brazil nuts are super-high in selenium so you should ration these crunchy numbers (too much selenium can be a bad thing for the body). That said, it's a mineral crucial for thyroid health, so the occasional Brazil nut is recommended.

ANNA139, JOHNER IMAGES, KEVIN SUMMERS, FLOORTJE, POPOVAPHOTO, 4KODIAK © GETTY IMAGES

YOU'LL NEED

2 cups wholemeal flour
1 tsp baking powder
pinch of salt
¼ cup wattleseed (roasted and ground)
1½ cups dried bush tomatoes
1 tbs ground lemon myrtle
½ cup sugar
1 cup milk
1 egg
7 tbs unsalted butter

ORIGINS

When modern Australia was born it started searching for symbols to hang its Akubra hat on. Wattle, which sets the land alight with a gorgeous glow each spring, became the floral emblem, and Wattle Day has been celebrated on 1 September ever since. Aboriginal people have used lemon myrtle and wattleseed to flavour food and make flour for centuries – it wasn't until the 1980s that native food guru Vic Cherikoff brought bush tucker to mainstream restaurant tables.

BAYSIDE © GETTY IMAGES. ASHLEY MACKEVICIUS © STOCKFOOD

AUSTRALIA

WATTLESEED, LEMON MYRTLE AND BUSH TOMATO MUFFINS

The seed of Australia's emblematic wattletree tastes like nothing else on earth. Wise to its flavoursome superpowers, Indigenous Australians have been eating it forever, but now it crops up in cool cakeshops and cafes countrywide.

METHOD

1 Sieve the flour, baking powder and salt into a big mixing bowl, add the wattleseed, bush tomatoes and lemon myrtle (saving a small bit of each), and mix thoroughly.

2 In a smaller bowl, combine the sugar, milk, eggs and butter and give it a good whisk.

3 Add the moist mixture to the dry ingredients in the big bowl, and stir them together until they're thoroughly combined.

4 Grease a 12-cup muffin pan and spoon in the mixture, filling each one about 75 per cent, sprinkle the leftover seed and myrtle over them, and then pop a bush tomato on top.

5 Place in an oven preheated to 180°C (350°F) and bake for 18–20 minutes, or until golden brown and cooked through. (Test if the muffins are ready by inserting a skewer – if it comes out clean, you're set.).

6 Take out of the oven and cool for 5 minutes before turning out the muffins on to a cooling rack or plate and serving warm or cold.

TIP *For a vegan version, replace milk with soy milk, the egg with 1 tablespoon of vinegar, and use ⅓ cup canola oil instead of butter.)*

TASTING NOTES

Australia's springtime starts with a rush, when wattle – an acacia that hides in plain sight for most of the year – suddenly sets every bit of scrubland and bush ablaze with explosions of lurid lemon-yellow flowers, brilliant contrasts to the brown earth and blue sky. Instantly life turns inside out, with social events revolving around backyard barbies, beach cricket and park picnics, where burgers and beers are best chased down by homemade wattleseed muffins. The exact flavour of this treat is tougher to tie down than a tickly kangaroo – if it were a wine, the label would wax lyrical about hints of nut, suggestions of chocolate and rumours of coffee – but it's undeniably delicious, and you'll be back like a boomerang for more. ● *by Patrick Kinsella*

ORIGINS

Native to southern Mexico and Central America, seeds of the bushy green chia plant have been prized as a superfood for thousands of years. Known as 'the running food', chia seeds mixed with water were a prime energy source for Aztec warriors, powering their conquests across the region. Today, the seeds, packed with protein, fibre and Omega 3 fatty acids, remain a popular addition to fruity drinks in Mexico and have also been adopted by the fitness fraternity worldwide.

WESTEND61, EGAL, © GETTY IMAGES

MEXICO AND CENTRAL AMERICA

CHIA FRESCA

MAKES 4 GLASSES

Hundreds of tiny mottled brown and grey chia seeds, each encased in a gelatinous film, add a pleasing texture and visual interest to this refreshing, power-boosting lemon drink.

YOU'LL NEED

- 1.4L (about 6 cups) cold water
- 4 large lemons (about 12 tbs of juice)
- 8 tsp sugar or sweetener of choice, such as maple or agave syrup.
- 4 tsp chia seeds

METHOD

1 Pour the water into a pitcher.

2 Roll each lemon firmly on the kitchen counter or table for about 10 seconds to help release the juices inside.

3 Slice the lemons in half and squeeze the juice into the water. Taste, then add more lemon juice if you prefer.

4 Stir in the sugar or sweetener. If using granulated sugar, dissolve it first in a little hot water before combining it with the other ingredients.

5 Stir the chia seeds into the liquid and let it sit in the fridge for around 10 minutes – enough time for the seeds to become gelatinous.

6 Before serving, stir the drink in the pitcher to evenly distribute the seeds.

7 If you like, you can also add slices of lemon to the pitcher or in each glass as a garnish.

TASTING NOTES

As chia seeds absorb liquid a gelatinous film is created around their surface - imagine something like frog's spawn or tomato seeds. That visual image might put you off, but the resulting concoction is very easy to swallow, with the drink going down smoothly. The seeds are entirely encased in their jelly coats so you get no crunch or taste to impair whatever flavour you also add to the water. Mexicans love to mix in lemon or lime juice, the tartness of which can be undercut with your sweetener of choice. It all adds up to a hyper-refreshing, energy-packed drink that looks as good as it tastes. ● *by Simon Richmond*

ORIGINS

The bliss balls' beginnings are a bit of a mystery, but it's likely that they evolved within the raw food or vegan diet movements, where they have been regarded as a highly prized treat for years.

Today, there are countless recipes and adaptations around the globe, thousands of which can be found online for you to try, adapt and adore. The only cause of upset? That you hadn't discovered them sooner!

YOU'LL NEED

¾ cup raw almonds
¼ cup raw cashews
1 cup Medjool dates
2 tbs raw cacao powder
pinch of salt
1 tbs water

TASTING NOTES

Although you could pop a whole bliss ball straight into your mouth, there is always an overwhelming desire to bite through one. And this feeling is the same, whether it's your first or fifth. Listen to your instincts – biting down into a bliss ball, cutting through the rich, nutty texture and sweet, date-derived moistness, is a sensation indeed. While your taste buds sing, your mind will struggle with a simple fact: no sugar or butter naughtiness is involved. Often found in cafes and health-minded eateries, these energising treats are great with an espresso prior to a gym session or as a treat after brunch on a lazy Sunday. ● *by Matt Phillips*

KINZIE RIEHM © GETTY IMAGES

MAKES ABOUT 14-20 BALLS

AUSTRALIA, CANADA, NEW ZEALAND, UK AND USA

CACAO, ALMOND AND CASHEW BLISS BALLS

Bliss balls – it's all in the name. These no-bake, easy-make balls of energy will have you enraptured from the first bite.

METHOD

1 Use a food processor to blitz the nuts.

2 Add the Medjool dates and blend again until mixed.

3 Add the cacao and salt, mixing again in the food processor.

4 Slowly add the water a little at a time until you have the right consistency (you may use less or more than the 1 tablespoon) – the balls should stick together, but be easy to roll.

5 Scoop up about a tablespoon of the mixture at a time, rolling each portion into a ball with your hands (if the mixture is sticking to your hands, wet them with a little water first).

6 You can choose to go off-piste here if you like, decorating the balls by rolling them in chia seeds or desiccated coconut. Goji berries can also be added to the mixture prior to rolling.

7 Place the balls in the freezer for about an hour, then store them in an airtight container in the fridge.

NATALITA ARZAMASOVA © GETTY IMAGES

ORIGINS

The texture of this ancient sweetmeat is said to recall the crude mud mortar that Jewish slaves were forced to prepare for the Pharaoh, rooting it firmly in the Passover legend, but this ancient palate primer is a joyous celebration of the flavours of the Levant. Every Jewish community takes its own liberties with texture and ingredients, but the core flavours of fruit, cinnamon and sweet wine shine through.

ISRAEL

CHAROSET

SERVES 4

Some rituals of Passover are as mysterious as the Old Testament itself, but everyone can get behind *charoset*, the revitalising fruit paste served at the famously high-spirited Passover *seder*.

YOU'LL NEED

1 apple, peeled, cored and diced
1 pear, peeled, cored and diced
½ cup dried raisins
1 cup walnuts, chopped
½ cup sweet red kosher wine
¼ tsp cinnamon
¼ tsp ground nutmeg

METHOD

1 First, decide if you want a smooth or chunky *charoset*; if you want it smooth, just blend the ingredients in a pestle and mortar or food processer at the end of the process.

2 Place the diced apple and pear in a bowl.

3 Add the raisins and chopped walnuts; if you can't find pre-chopped walnuts, finely chop walnut halves.

4 Mix together the kosher wine and spices and pour over the mixture.

5 Refrigerate the *charoset* for at least an hour to let the flavours steep.

6 Serve with bitter horseradish or romaine lettuce leaves and *matzah* flatbread.

TASTING NOTES

On your first encounter with *charoset*, expect hints of apple, wine, and nutty tones of walnut. So, basically, the natural bounty that grows along every village lane in the Levant. It's a sweet, luxurious counterpoint to the medicinal bitterness of the *maror* – the 'bitter herbs' demanded by the Book of Exodus – and the dry crispness of *matzah* flatbread. Ben & Jerry's even celebrated this millennia-old sweetmeat with a dedicated ice-cream flavour, made kosher of course, to earn a place at the *seder* table. The taste of *charoset* is only enhanced by the elaborate, protracted ceremonies that precede its arrival. After seemingly endless rounds of chanting and rituals, it is the *charoset* that breaks the ice, wakes the dozing relatives and compels the feast to begin! ● *by Joe Bindloss*

BRIAN HAGIWARA © GETTY IMAGES

ORIGINS

The cocoa bean was first cultivated by the Mayans over 3000 years ago. They believed the beans had divine origins, even using them as currency. *Shamen* (Mayan medicine men) also used cacao in healing rituals. When they created their chocolate drink, sugar wasn't yet available, so it was a bitter concoction spiced with chilli, cinnamon and vanilla and served cold. Aztecs also loved the drink: emperor Montezuma reputedly consumed 50 cups a day.

SERVES 1

MEXICO

RAW CACAO HOT CHOCOLATE

The raw cacao version of arguably the most decadent warm drink out there, fragranced with cayenne and cinnamon, allows you to dose up on its antioxidant goodness with zero guilt and maximum rewards.

YOU'LL NEED

1 cup almond milk, rice milk or oat milk, depending on preference (cows' milk is also possible)
1 tbs raw cacao powder
1 tsp cinnamon
1 tsp vanilla extract
pinch of cayenne pepper (optional)
1 tsp coconut sugar

METHOD

1 Add the milk, cacao, cinnamon, vanilla extract and cayenne pepper to a pan and warm.

2 Remove the pan from the heat before it reached boiling point.

3 Sweeten as required with the coconut sugar. Drink up!

TIP *The Mayans ground the cocoa seeds into a paste then mixed this with water, corn meal and spices to make what they considered an aphrodisiac elixir. Pouring it back and forth between two pitchers ensured it developed a satisfying froth.*

TASTING NOTES

The homely, earthy feel of the traditional sturdy terracotta mugs used to serve hot chocolate in Mexico enhances the cosy sensation of sipping on a cup of cocoa. Its deep, sultry chocolate notes never fail to revive body and spirit while its velvety texture is undeniably soothing. Stop at one of Mexico City's sleek cafes for a mug accompanied with some *pan dulce* (sweet breads) when you need a restorative pick-me-up from sightseeing or enjoy it Mayan-style as part of a shamanic raw-cacao healing ceremony. Imagine a dark night on a tranquil beach in the Yucatán peninsula, lit by a campfire and a full moon as your *shamen* (medicine man) hands round medicinal-strength hot cacao elixirs while performing blessings designed to promote euphoria and open the heart. ● *by Helen Brown*

LIUBOVLEVA © GETTY IMAGES

ORIGINS

Tahini is the oily paste you get from heavily grinding sesame seeds. The recipe's roots in the Middle East are clear from its name, which is believed to derive from the Arabic word meaning to grind. It's an ancient superfood, Greek historian Herodotus having noted some 3500 years ago the cultivation of sesame around the Tigris and Euphrates rivers (modern-day Iraq) and its use as a source of oil.

MAKES
1 CUP

TAHINI

This creamy, nutty sauce made from ground sesame seeds can be enjoyed on its own as well as in dishes such as hummus and baba ganoush.

YOU'LL NEED

1½ cups hulled sesame seeds
2–3 tbs mild olive oil,
  grapeseed oil, and/or a
  small amount of sesame oil
salt (optional)

METHOD

1 Gently toast the raw sesame seeds in a dry pan over a medium heat, stirring them frequently with a wooden spoon until they are lightly coloured (not brown) and fragrant, about 5 minutes.

2 Transfer the toasted sesame seeds to a large plate or tray and let them cool completely.

3 Tip the seeds into a food processor, or you can use a mortar and pestle. Grind for 2–3 minutes until the seeds form a crumbly paste.

4 Add a couple of tablespoons of oil and continue grinding until the mixture forms a thick and fairly smooth paste.

5 For a thinner tahini, add more oil, 1–2 tablespoons at a time, and process until the desired consistency is reached.

6 Add salt to taste.

TASTING NOTES

While its ingredients and preparation are very simple, tahini can vary a lot depending on a number of factors. Your first choice is whether to go for hulled sesame seeds – the ones that are a pale creamy colour – or the darker ones with their outer shells intact. Use of unhulled seeds can provide a richer flavour but it can also make the tahini slightly bitter and gritty. You can also decide whether to toast or not toast the seeds before grinding (toasting brings out the nutty flavour), and how smooth you prefer the sauce to be. Consider the origin of the sesame seeds, too: the Ethiopian variety *humera* is preferred by cooks for its sweetness.

● *by Simon Richmond*

ANDREW MONTGOMERY © LONELY PLANET, GIGORDINHAN © 4CORNERS, ALEXPRO9500 © GETTY IMAGES

PATRIZIA SAVARESE © GETTY IMAGES

LEGUMES

Already known and loved by vegetarians and vegans as high-protein meat substitutes (particularly soybeans), legumes should definitely be embraced by everyone, not only for their health benefits but also for their incredible variety (13,000 different kinds!) and versatility. From the more popular lentils and chickpeas to the lesser-known power of licorice root, legumes can transcend any associations with dullness or uninspired eating. In fact, we're calling them a sexy superfood; after all, they're packed with nutrients that provide an immediate mood boost. And don't we all need some of that. →

HISTORY

Legumes have been around since before 6000 BC and were one of the earliest domesticated plants in the New World. Along with cereals (p56), legumes were the first to be found preserved in archaeological sites. Because legumes are one of the highest-protein plant foods, they were also traditionally associated with poverty and were chosen by people who could not afford to eat meat. That said, however, the fact that this food choice was high in protein was probably more of a 'happy accident' than the result of any knowledge or forethought. Perhaps in those days, people could focus more on what felt right for their bodies rather than being bombarded by advertising!

HEALTH BENEFITS

Daily legume consumption leads to improvement in blood circulation and also significantly reduces cholesterol levels, which means a much healthier heart. Legumes have the lowest glycaemic index of any food group, making them ideal for diabetics or anyone watching blood-sugar levels. With complex carbohydrates, protein and (soluble and insoluble) fibre, legumes also keep you fuller for longer on less calories, with regular, healthy bowel movements (come on, we had to say this somewhere). Those who use legumes as a meat replacement will know they are a cheaper alternative and, unlike meat, are cholesterol-free with very little saturated fat.

PEATHEGEE INC. CULTURA RM EXCLUSIVE/GARY LATHAM © GETTY IMAGES

BRETT STEVENS; MAXIMILIAN STOCK LTD. © GETTY IMAGES

DID YOU KNOW?

Let's get the terminology out of the way: beans are legumes but not all legumes are beans. A legume is a plant that has a pod that bears fruit. A pulse is part of the legume family but the term 'pulse' refers only to the dried seed. If you're shrewd enough to know a peanut is actually a legume, you'll find it masquerading as a nut (for ease of reference) in the Seeds & Nuts section (p12).

VARIANTS

Take your pick: dried, tinned or fresh. The jury is still out on whether soaking dried legumes overnight prior to cooking is strictly necessary, although it does shorten the cooking time by softening the skins, and enhances nutrient absorption by making them more digestible. However, a recent article (January 2016) in the *New York Times* suggested that spontaneous cooks (without sensitive stomachs) can bypass the overnight soaking and just cook the legumes for longer. If you'd rather not soak them, there are also plenty of tinned, pre-cooked varieties available to purchase (just watch the salt levels). Some legumes, such as peas and fava beans, can be eaten fresh in spring and summer.

BEANS

The humble baked bean (also known as a haricot or navy bean) in your breakfast fry-up can be a wonderful thing. But the commercial variety smothered in a sugary, salty tomato sauce is not the kind of superfood we're talking about here. Beans can be your friend, not just at breakfast but in any meal: think kidney beans in chilli, soybeans in miso soup. Give them the proper focus and you'll see how much they can surreptitiously add to your diet.

SOYBEANS

The most super of the beans (see boxed text, opposite top), soybeans come from the soya plant and are the richest dietary source of phytoestrogens, with researchers suggesting they help prevent cancer, cardiovascular disease and osteoporosis.

CHICKPEAS (AKA GARBANZO BEANS)

High in protein and fibre, low in fat, chickpeas grow on trees and are the secret behind every great hummus dip (p50). There are three different kinds (two types harvested in India, another from Europe/Africa), though all have the same health benefits.

KIDNEY BEANS

Small red kidney beans contain more antioxidants than fresh blueberries (p81) and are an excellent source of the mineral molybdenum, known to detoxify sulphites (a salty preservative commonly added to prepared foods). White kidney beans are known as cannellini beans.

SCIENCE PHOTO LIBRARY, ALASDAIR THOMSON, DIANAZH © GETTY IMAGES

JUAN MOYANO, YODASWAJ; PICTUREPARTNERS © GETTY IMAGES

WHAT'S ALL THE FUSS ABOUT SOYBEANS?

Yes, soybeans are more special than other beans. Other legumes will only provide a complete protein when they are eaten together (or at least on the same day) with whole grains (p61): they're known as 'complementary proteins'. Soybeans, however – alone, by themselves, without anyone else's help, thank you, whole grains – contain all nine essential amino acids, forming a complete protein.

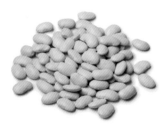

BROAD BEANS (AKA FAVA BEANS)

Some associate fava beans with *The Silence of the Lambs'* Hannibal Lecter (we discuss liver, p144), but our intentions are purely virtuous. Containing levodopa (a precursor of brain neurochemicals), they may help prevent Parkinson's disease.

MUNG BEANS

Small, oval and green, mung beans are a great source of potassium, which prevents kidney stones, lowers heart-disease risk and reduces blood pressure. Also rich in iron (good for energy) and magnesium (an energy booster, but also maintains muscle health).

LIMA BEANS

Like kidney beans, lima beans are a rich source of molybdenum, as well as being high in fibre, folate and magnesium, the latter three of which are beneficial to heart health. They're sometimes also called 'butter beans' because of their starchy, buttery texture.

OTHER LEGUMES

LENTILS

A powerhouse of lean protein, fibre, iron and folate, lentils come in a variety of colours: red, green, orange, black and white. The French green ones (also known as Puy lentils) are the most expensive, though many consider them the best for their peppery flavour and ability to hold their shape during cooking.

PEAS

Fresh green peas a superfood? Yes, indeed. Recent research shows that one of their phytonutrients (coumestrol) can reduce the risk of stomach cancer. Peas are also excellent for the digestive system, can help lower cholesterol with their high fibre content, and are a great source of Vitamins A and C, iron and folate.

ALFALFA

Once typically used to feed cattle, alfalfa sprouts have played a role in herbal medicine (notably traditional Chinese medicine) for 1500 years. They are a nourishing and preventative food, thought to protect against cardiovascular disease and nervous-system deterioration and to slow the onset of osteoporosis.

MANUELA WESCHKE: REDHELGA; ANTIMARTINA © GETTY IMAGES

HOW TO COOK LEGUMES

Tinned legumes just need reheating, and cook quickly. For dried legumes, the simplest and best way is to simmer them in a pan of salted water with perhaps some herbs and vegetables for flavour, until tender. If stored in a cool, dry place, dried legumes can keep almost indefinitely, though the longer they're stored, the more difficult it is to tenderise them during cooking. Try to use them within a year.

LICORICE ROOT

Used as a medicinal herb since 500 BC, notably for treatment of peptic ulcer disease, coughs, constipation and blood-sugar disorders, licorice root is much more than a sweet treat. Researchers have confirmed its anti-inflammatory and antimicrobial properties. It is also reported to protect against prostate cancer.

SCIENCE PHOTO LIBRARY © GETTY IMAGES, SIMON URWIN © LONELY PLANET

YOU'LL NEED

For kushari

¼ cup olive oil
3 yellow onions, peeled and
    sliced into thin rings
1 cup basmati rice
2 cups of water
1 bay leaf
1 cup cooked brown lentils
1 cup cooked macaroni
salt and ground black pepper,
    to taste
1 cup cooked chickpeas

For tomato sauce

1 onion, peeled and finely
    chopped
2 garlic cloves, peeled and
    crushed
2 tbs olive oil
½ tsp ground black pepper
1 tsp ground cumin
½ tsp ground coriander
3 cloves, ground
¼ tsp ground cardamom
½ tsp ground cinnamon
½ tsp ground paprika
1½ cups tomato puree
2 tsp white vinegar
salt to taste
chilli flakes to taste

ORIGINS

Kushari goes back about 200 years, born in Egypt but probably developed from an Indian dish. It's become a multicultural affair, with an ingredients list that spans the globe: pasta, pulses, rice, tomatoes. But the deep charm of this spectacular dish lies in its flexibility. This is not a strict recipe, and if you use a bit more of that and a little less of this – after all, that's how you make it a family classic.

TASTING NOTES

Big. Bold. It's just so flavourful and satisfying. Each mouthful is a smash of textures, the dense meatiness of the chickpeas, the subtle bite of the lentils, the crispy fried onions, the soft rice and pasta. Then the flavours do their dance, with the tang of the tomato and vinegar sauce, the deep, layered warmth of the spices. It's not to say that healthy eating isn't delicious eating, but *kushari* is as delicious as a dish can be. You'll leave your empty plate with a smile, full and still wanting more, guaranteed. All this and more if you can find your way to Egypt and enjoy it from the hands of a street vendor! ● *by Ben Handicott*

SIMON REDDY © ALAMY

SERVES 4

EGYPT

KUSHARI

There's superfood, and then there's SUPER food. *Kushari* is both; healthy and all that (what, with lentils, chickpeas and tomato), but oh... the taste! The satisfaction! It's healthy eating for those who usually let pleasure dictate their menu.

METHOD

For kushari

1 Heat the oil in a large pan over a medium heat and add the sliced onions. Cook until they are caramelized to a deep brown – don't let them burn though!

2 Remove the onions from the pan and set aside.

3 Add the rice to the pan and fry for a couple of minutes.

4 Add the water and bay leaf to the pan, bring to the boil, then turn the heat down and let the rice cook till soft.

5 Add the cooked lentils and macaroni to the rice and gently combine.

6 Season the mixture with salt and pepper to taste and spoon out on to a serving dish.

7 Top the *kushari* with the chickpeas and fried onions and pour the tomato sauce over the top.

8 Serve with a side salad and flat bread if you feel like making a meal of it.

For tomato sauce

1 Gently fry the onion and garlic in the oil for 5 minutes.

2 Add the spices (and chilli flakes if using), mix together and cook for 2 minutes.

3 Add the tomato puree and vinegar and gently simmer for 20 minutes.

4 Season with salt and chilli flakes to taste.

JONATHAN GREGSON © LONELY PLANET

YOU'LL NEED

400g (14oz) mung dhal
  (skinned yellow split mung
  beans)
2L (8 cups) vegetable stock
4 garlic cloves, peeled and
  crushed
4cm (1½in) piece of ginger,
  peeled and cut into quarters
1 tbs turmeric powder
2 small green chillies, finely
  chopped and deseeded (if
  liked)
1 tsp salt
2 tbs ghee
2 French shallots, peeled and
  finely sliced
1 tbs cumin seeds
1 tsp mustard seeds
1 tsp chilli flakes
juice of 1 lemon or 2 limes
3 handfuls of coriander leaves
  (cilantro), chopped, to serve
cooked rice or flatbreads to
  serve

ORIGINS

Technically the word 'dhal'
means 'split' in Sanskrit.
Yet, while the dish is often made
with split lentils, the term has
come to signify all dried peas
and beans. It has been part of
India's daily diet since before
6000 BC, long before rice even
arrived in India. Ancient texts
say the dish was served at celebrations such as the marriage
of Helen of Troy to Chadragupta
Maurya in 303 BC. The mung
bean version is particularly
popular in southern India.

MUKESH-KUMAR; NICHOLAS DEVORE © GETTY IMAGES

INDIA

MUNG TARKA DHAL

SERVES 6

This mild curry is a staple of the Indian diet. Often prescribed as part of the ayurvedic healing system, it fuses protein and fibre-rich mung beans with medicinal spices such as cumin, ginger, turmeric and cardamom.

METHOD

1 Rinse the mung beans until the water runs clear.

2 Put the mung beans in a pan and cover with the vegetable stock.

3 Bring the stock to the boil, removing any residue that appears on the surface.

4 Add the garlic, ginger, turmeric, chopped chillies and a pinch of salt to the pan. Partially cover the pan with a lid, and simmer over a low heat for about 1½ hours, stirring occasionally, until the dhal has broken down and developed a creamy consistency.

5 Add boiling water or reduce the dhal further to achieve your preferred consistency, then season to taste with more salt, if necessary.

6 Next, make the *tarka* (the spice mix that is drizzled over the finished dhal to make it explode with flavour). Heat the ghee in a frying pan over a medium heat, then add the shallots and stir-fry until golden.

7 Add the cumin and mustard seeds and the chilli flakes and cook for a couple of minutes until the mustard seeds are beginning to pop.

8 Tip the *tarka* and the lemon or lime juice over the dhal, stir in, and top with chopped coriander.

9 Serve with rice or flatbreads.

TASTING NOTES

There is something undeniably meditative about this gentle comfort food: whether you are enjoying it in the peaceful environs of a Keralan ayurvedic retreat as you gaze on to the backwaters, or seated on a plastic stool by a Delhi street-food shack as *tuk tuks* hurtle past and cows plod by, it has the ability to calm and ground. Its creaminess, achieved by churning the mixture with a wooden tool called a *mathani* or through a super-slow cooking process, is crucial to its heartwarming nature. An integral part of any *thali* (an Indian meal composed of a selection of dishes), the softly aromatic mix is especially sumptuous soaked up with a paratha (flatbread) or spooned over rice, being full-bodied enough to interest the taste buds while retaining its soothing feel. ● *by Helen Brown*

ORIGINS

Legend has it that a beautiful but unhappy bride named Ezo attempted to impress her future mother-in-law by cooking this soup, hence the name Ezogelin ('Ezo, the bride'). References to red lentil soup and its soothing properties can be found in Turkish medicinal manuscripts, as far back as the 14th century. Prepared with unripe grape juice or vinegar, or even chicken meat, the soup was deemed a cure for everything from headaches to the flu and smallpox.

TURKEY

EZOGELIN ÇORBASI

SERVES 4

This slightly spicy and satisfyingly heart-warming orange-hued lentil soup is a popular and nutritious way to start the day in Turkey, served with hunks of warm *pide* (bread).

YOU'LL NEED

1 tbs butter
1 tsp flour
1 tbs tomato paste
1 tbs red pepper paste (or an equal quantity of additional tomato paste)
1 tbs dried mint
1 tsp red pepper flakes (or an equal quantity of hot paprika), plus extra to serve
1 cup red lentils, washed but not soaked
⅓ cup bulgur wheat
5 cups vegetable stock
lemon wedges, to serve

METHOD

1 Melt the butter in a large pan over a medium heat.

2 Stir in the flour to make a paste.

3 Cook the flour paste, stirring, for 1 minute.

4 Stir in the tomato paste, red pepper paste, dried mint and red pepper flakes.

5. Cook, stirring, for 2 minutes.

6 Add the red lentils, bulgur wheat and stock and bring to the boil.

7 Reduce the heat to low and simmer for 20–30 minutes, stirring occasionally, until the lentils are soft.

8 Serve immediately with a squeeze of lemon and extra red pepper flakes to taste.

TASTING NOTES

As a breakfast item or afternoon snack in Turkey, *Ezogelin çorbası* is light and delicately flavoured with just enough kick from the distinctive red pepper flakes, an indigenous condiment found all over Turkey that is used to season most foods in the same way as salt and pepper are employed elsewhere. The addition of chunks of tomato and other flavourful spices, a popular way of preparing the soup in Anatolia, makes for a hearty and satisfying meal in its own right. Hot from the soup pot, soft lentils and cracked bulgur wheat give an earthy, mealy texture while the quintessential Turkish triumvirate flavourings of dried mint, red pepper paste and red pepper flakes lend the soup a uniquely aromatic and exotic character, which is virtually impossible to replicate with substitute ingredients. ● *by Johanna Ashby*

MARK READ; MATT MUNRO © LONELY PLANET; GRÄFE & UNZER VERLAG / NICOLE STICH © STOCKFOOD

BOAZ ROTTEM © ALAMY

ORIGINS

Egyptians have enjoyed broad beans since the time of the Pharaohs. At the end of each day, cooks placed tureens of beans upon the embers of smouldering fires at bath houses to slowly cook overnight into a flavourful stew. Egyptians so revered these beans that they also offered them to the gods. The recipe was exported across the Middle East and Africa. Today, *ful medames* is considered a national dish of Egypt.

YOU'LL NEED

250g (9oz) dried broad beans
5 garlic cloves
½ cup olive oil
juice of 1 lemon
¼ tsp cumin
½ tsp coriander powder
1 cup water
4 eggs
4 pita
tahini and extra olive oil, to serve (optional)
4 parsley sprigs, to garnish

TASTING NOTES

Even in frenetic Cairo, not everything happens in a hurry. And there's certainly no rushing a good *ful medames*. Before the city's chorus of car horns reaches a climax, when the early-morning fog is still draped over skyscrapers and minarets, Cairenes drift towards street vendors for a plateful. So follow the crowds (and your nose) when you choose a spot for breakfast. Liberal drizzlings of olive oil add to the rich, smoky flavour of the *ful*, which is best eaten by hand. Scoop it up with rounds of freshly baked bread, and cleanse your palate with pickled vegetables. '*Laziza*' (delicious) might be difficult to say with a mouthful of bread and *ful*, but your appreciative murmurs are sure to breach the language barrier. ● *by Anita Isalska*

EGYPT

FUL MEDAMES

From street corners to five-star restaurants, Egyptians breakfast on a dish that has barely changed since 2000 BC: slow-cooked spiced broad beans loaded on to stone-baked flatbread.

METHOD

1 Soak the dried beans in a large bowl of cold water, ideally for about 12 hours.

2 Once the beans are plumped up with water, peel and crush the garlic cloves.

3 Heat the olive oil in a large frying pan.

4 Add the garlic, drained beans, lemon juice, cumin and coriander to the olive oil.

5 Stir the mixture over a low heat for 5 minutes, until the ingredients are well mixed and heated through.

6 Pour the contents of the pan into a slow-cooker.

7 Add the water and leave the cooker on a low heat for about 12 hours (ideally overnight, so you can enjoy your *ful* in the morning). Stir occasionally.

8 In the morning, hard-boil the eggs in a pan of boiling water for 4 minutes.

9 Remove the eggs from the pan with a slotted spoon and place them straight into a bowl of cool water.

10 Allow the eggs to cool slightly, then peel off the shells.

11 Slice the hard-boiled eggs into quarters.

12 Toast the pita under a grill for 2 minutes on each side.

13 Place one pita on each of four plates.

14 Place a ladleful of the slow-cooked beans next to each pita.

15 Drizzle the remaining olive oil on each serving of *ful*.

16 Top each portion with a small sprig of parsley and four egg quarters.

TIP *Using a slow-cooker is the best way to replicate the ancient method of making* ful medames, *and it ensures thorough infusion of the spices. However, if you're short on time, boil the soaked beans for 1 hour before draining and mashing in the spices.*

LISA LINDER © GETTY IMAGES. MICHAEL HEFFERNAN © LONELY PLANET

ORIGINS

Harira's origin dates back centuries in Morocco, with the soup's recipe evolving from family to family. Variations can be as subtle as the inclusion of paprika and cumin, or as strong as the addition of *smen*, a fermented butter with an almost blue-cheese flavour. While most people prefer the consistency to be velvety smooth, some recipes thicken the soup into a stew with rice or broken vermicelli. Its popularity has now spread throughout the Muslim world.

YOU'LL NEED

2 tbs butter
450g (1lb) diced lamb
1½ tsp ground black pepper
1 tsp ground turmeric
1 tsp ground cinnamon
¼ tsp ground ginger
¼ tsp ground cayenne pepper
90g (about one stick) celery, chopped
1 yellow onion, peeled and chopped
1 red onion, peeled and chopped
25g (¼ cup) fresh coriander (cilantro), chopped
800g (28oz) tomatoes, chopped
1.7L (6½ cups) water
145g (5oz) dried green lentils, rinsed and drained
410g (14oz) chickpeas, rinsed and drained
115g (4oz) spaghetti
2 eggs, beaten
juice of 1 lemon

SERVES 6

MOROCCO

MOROCCO

HARIRA

Moroccans en masse reach for *harira* to break each fasting day of Ramadan for good reason. This soup, laden with chickpeas, lentils and tomatoes, is as healthy as it is hearty.

METHOD

1 Melt the butter in a large soup pot. Add the diced lamb, black pepper, turmeric, cinnamon, ginger, cayenne, celery, onion and coriander and stir frequently for 5 minutes until the lamb is browned.

2 Add the tomatoes and simmer for 15 minutes.

3 Add the water and lentils. Bring to a boil, then reduce the heat. Cover and simmer for two hours.

4 Turn the heat to medium-high about 10 minutes prior to serving and add the chickpeas and spaghetti (and more water if the mixture is too thick; it should be velvety).

5 After 10 minutes, stir in the beaten egg and lemon, and cook for an additional minute. The eggs should form white streaks.

6 Remove from the heat and serve.

TASTING NOTES

The daily drama and *halqa* (street theatre) in Djemaa el-Fna, Marrakesh's main square, usually subsides each evening when the countless chefs arrive to start preparing dinner for the thousands, but during Ramadan a different story plays out. Quiet crowds of Moroccans gather round large cooking vats full of *hariria*, each person seemingly counting the seconds till sunset. Even if you'd had a large lunch, the fragrant smells of cinnamon, turmeric and pepper emanating from the soup as it's stirred are enough to make your stomach grumble. When the flood of eating begins, grab a bowl and tuck in to this zesty and warming meal. It's traditionally served with crusty bread and eaten with a *taghanjat* (wooden spoon). ● *by Matt Phillips*

ALPEG © GETTY IMAGES

ORIGINS

Hummus comes from the Middle East, but exactly when and where it developed no one is sure. Chickpeas were cultivated in Neolithic times, and Arab recipes from the Middle Ages mention ways of preparing them but, according to one scholar, the first batch of hummus as we know it was boiled up in 18th-century Damascus. Whatever the case, hummus is hugely popular all over the Levant and is revered among both Jews and Arabs.

YOU'LL NEED

250g (9oz) dried chickpeas
5 cups water, for cooking the chickpeas
½ tsp bicarb soda (baking soda)(optional)
½ cup tahini (sesame-seed paste)
¼ cup freshly squeezed lemon juice
2 garlic cloves, peeled and crushed
½ tbs salt
fresh pita, to serve

Optional toppings
extra virgin olive oil
chopped fresh parsley
pickle slices
ground cumin
sweet paprika
ground black pepper
pine nuts

Optional to serve
diced hard-boiled egg
falafel
s'chug (Yemenite chilli paste)
thick slices of white onion

TASTING NOTES

Hummus inspires passions, and many connoisseurs have ardent views about the right way to prepare and serve it. Some like theirs as smooth and creamy as mousse, others prefer it textured and a little bit rough. Israelis enjoy 'wiping up' hummus with a pita at any time of the day or night, but for Palestinians, Jordanians and Lebanese hummus is commonly eaten for breakfast or brunch, often in little eateries that close by mid-afternoon. If you want to get Arabs and Israelis to agree about something, though, casually suggest making the beloved paste with peanut butter instead of tahini (as one celebrity chef does) – disbelief will quickly be replaced by a united chorus of outrage and disgust! ● *by Daniel Robinson*

LEBANON, JORDAN, ISRAEL AND PALESTINE

HUMMUS

Try not to let the oil drip as you scoop up a dab of smooth hummus with a piece of warm pita and bring the lemony, garlicky morsel to your lips – chickpea superfood heaven!

METHOD

1 Remove any damaged, misshapen or discoloured chickpeas. Rinse and then soak the chickpeas in a large bowl of cold water for 24 hours (in hot weather, place the bowl in the fridge to avoid fermentation). Change the water after 12 hours.

2 Drain and rinse the chickpeas before putting them in a large pan with the 5 cups of water over a high heat.

3 If you'd like your hummus to be creamy (rather than textured), add the bicarb soda.

4 When the mixture is boiling, skim off any foam. Reduce the heat to medium and cook the chickpeas 2–3 hours (in a pressure cooker, cook for 45 minutes after the contents start boiling).

5 Add water to ensure the chickpeas always remain covered with liquid.

6 Stir every 30 minutes so the mixture doesn't stick to the pan.

7 The chickpeas are ready when they squash easily between your thumb and index finger. Let the chickpeas cool in the water, then drain the chickpeas, setting aside 1 cup of the cooking liquid.

8 If you'd like to garnish the hummus with whole chickpeas, set aside ½ cup of the cooked chickpeas.

9 Put the chickpeas, tahini, lemon juice, crushed garlic and salt in a blender and puree for at least 3 minutes. If the mixture is too thick, add cooking liquid as required to achieve your preferred consistency.

10 Using a circular motion, spread the now-creamy hummus in a shallow bowl so that it is evenly distributed along the bottom and sides.

11 Garnish the hummus with your preferred combination of toppings. Serve the hummus with fresh pita (for scooping up the hummus) and, if you'd like, diced hard-boiled egg, felafel, *s'chug* (Yemenite hot chilli paste) and/or thick slices of onion.

YOU'LL NEED

1 tbs dried wakame seaweed
350g (12oz) firm/soft tofu
4 cups water
1 (5g) sachet *bonito dashi* stock
2 tbs miso paste
1 spring onion (scallion), sliced

ORIGINS

Originating in China in the 4th century, miso was introduced to Japan in the 7th century by Buddhist monks. The hearty soup's fortifying nature has long been revered: it was a mainstay of the samurai warrior's diet and helped manual labourers to work long hours even when animal protein was scarce. In Tokyo, miso soup is referred to as *omiotsuke*, a term that contains three words that signify respect (o, mi, and o), an accolade that no other food achieves.

JON ARNOLD; CULTURA RM EXCLUSIVE/BRETT STEVENS © GETTY IMAGES

JAPAN

MISO SOUP

Japan's ubiquitous broth made from fermented soybeans dissolved in a seaweed and fish-based *dashi* (stock) is love in liquid form to the nation. Warming, salty and soothing, it never fails to comfort.

METHOD

1 Rehydrate the wakame by placing it in a bowl of cold water.

2 Chop the tofu into 1cm (½in) cubes

3 Put the water and *dashi* stock in a saucepan and gently bring to the boil.

4 Ladle a small amount of the stock into a bowl and add the miso paste, stirring it so that it does not go lumpy.

5 Add the wakame and tofu to the stock in the saucepan.

6 Take the stock off the heat before adding the dissolved miso (this helps retain the flavour of the miso and preserves its beneficial bacteria).

7 Stir the soup to keep it smooth as you add the miso.

8 Pour into bowls and top each with some slices of spring onion.

TASTING NOTES

According to Japanese mythology, miso is a gift from the gods to ensure health, happiness and longevity. So it's no surprise that it's served at almost every meal from breakfast through to dinner, often arriving in its traditional lacquer bowl even when it hasn't specifically been ordered. Slurping the salty solution from the edge of the bowl is encouraged whatever the setting, be it the privacy of your *ryokan* bedroom as you start your day with a resplendent Japanese breakfast platter, the sleek minimalist confines of a (fine-dining) restaurant or the local sushi bar. Swirl it around with your chopsticks to awaken the seaweed and tofu resting at the bottom. Flit between the soup and your other dishes as it's polite and ensures you maximise the broth's digestive benefits. ● *by Helen Brown*

YOU'LL NEED

113g (4oz) black quinoa, rinsed
2 tbs canola or peanut oil
2 tbs fresh root ginger,
 minced
225g (8oz) tempeh, cubed
100–150g (4–5oz) kale,
 chopped
1 chilli, chopped (or dried
 chilli flakes, to taste)
juice of ½ lemon

ORIGINS

This dish is a relatively modern invention, given that its constituent ingredients couldn't come together without globalised trade and culinary trends. To be fair, tempeh is from Indonesia and the Dutch love *boerenkool* (curly kale), and a history of Dutch colonialism *could* have brought the two ingredients together. But throwing South American quinoa into the mix is a distinctly 21st century innovation, and it's the sort of combination that bespeaks a marked Pacific Rim origination.

AMY HUNTER © TINY RED KITCHEN, MARK READ © LONELY PLANET

SERVES 2

CALIFORNIA, USA

TEMPEH WITH SPICY KALE AND BLACK QUINOA

If superfoods were weather patterns, this dish ploughs straight into a perfect storm – the leafy goodness of kale, the firm earthy bite of tempeh, the comforting starchiness of quinoa.

METHOD

1 Put the quinoa in a saucepan, cover with water and bring to the boil.

2 Stir, then reduce the heat to medium and simmer for 15 minutes, until the quinoa is cooked but still retains some firmness.

3 In a deep pan, heat the oil over a medium-high heat.

4 Add the ginger and tempeh to the oil. Cook for about 1 minute until the tempeh sizzles and starts to turn brown.

5 Add the kale, chilli and cooked quinoa. Stir-fry for about 5–7 minutes, until the kale has cooked a little, but has not totally wilted.

6 Add the lemon juice.

TASTING NOTES

Black quinoa and tempeh have strong notes of *terroir* – these are earthy ingredients, their solid musk cut by a hint of sweetness. Combined with kale's fragrant bitterness, this dish, minus any spicy heat, is surprisingly hearty, if not heavy. But throw in some fire and this recipe takes on a whole new texture. Fresh chillies add a fruity heat element that lightens the package, while dried chilli flakes are more one-dimensional, but still nicely undercuts the soily sweet and bitter base. A little ginger provides a nice refreshing zing, as does a squeeze of lemon juice. If you'd rather add some *umami* (pleasant savoury taste) depth, toss in a dash of *nuoc mam* (fish sauce). ● *by Adam Karlin*

MAXIMILIAN STOCK LTD. © GETTY IMAGES

GRAINS & CEREALS

Put all thoughts of processed, sugary, high-salt, boxed cereals aside. We're interested in the real, untouched, pure deal here. The terms 'grain' and 'cereal' both refer to the same thing: grasses that are cultivated from edible fruit seeds. And while wheat, rice, oats and barley were forever the main contenders in the grain group of the Healthy Food Pyramid, there are some new grains shaking things up in the superfood world. Or, rather, some ancient grains are back in town. And guess what: they're even better for you. →

HISTORY

Grains and cereals, like legumes (p32), were pretty much worshipped by ancient civilisations. The Aztecs, the Greeks, the Egyptians, the Romans, as well as African and Asian tribes had them as a staple part of their diet. Wheat was the first cereal to be cultivated by humans. It was seen as an important step forward in the hunter-gatherer mentality, because of the technical complexity required to turn such a raw material into a food staple. Relatively recent evidence of grass seed residue from the Middle Stone Age on some ancient African tools has got scientists thinking that grains date back even earlier than previously thought: over 100,000 years.

HEALTH BENEFITS

Grains and cereals tick a lot of healthy boxes: carbohydrates, protein, polyunsaturated fats, B-group vitamins, minerals and antioxidants. Whole grains and cereals have long had a close association with heart health – eating cereals rich in soluble fibre (especially oats and barley) can significantly reduce blood-cholesterol levels. Whole grains also contain many protective phytochemicals that assist in lowering cholesterol, but can ward off many other diseases and illnesses. For example, phytic acid reduces the glycaemic level of food (good news for diabetics) and helps protect against colon cancer. Studies have also shown that eating whole-grain foods daily can reduce the risk of developing Type 2 diabetes.

ALEX TREADWAY; WESTEND61 © GETTY IMAGES; PORTLAND PHOTOGRAPHY © STOCKFOOD

VARIANTS

The superfoods we're covering here are specifically whole grains (see boxed text, p61). There are plenty of other, lesser grains and cereals on the market, so be warned: some grains and cereals just aren't good for you. In fact, eating a diet high in refined cereals can increase your risk of developing Type 2 diabetes and some types of cancers (bowel, stomach, kidney). Refined cereals (found in white flour, white bread, pasta, white rice, cakes, desserts, muffins, pizza and sweet or savoury biscuits), which lack the grain's bran and germ, may be fine for the occasional indulgence or sweet treat, but consuming them on a too-regular basis can adversely affect the body.

DID YOU KNOW?

While it's often referred to as an 'ancient grain', quinoa isn't a grain or cereal. It's a pseudo-cereal: that is, a 'non-grass' seed (all cereals are grasses) that is cooked and treated like a grain. This also means that, unlike most cereals that contain wheat, it's gluten-free.

GLUTEN GRAINS & CEREALS

Given the rise of gluten-free awareness, an unfortunate side effect has been the belief that wheat is somehow evil. It's not. Sticking to whole wheat (not refined) is fine for those without dietary sensitivities. Also, gluten is present not just in wheat but also in many other very healthy grains. If you don't have any gluten issues, you would be missing out on some nutritious (and also tasty) meals if you avoided the superfoods below.

OATS

Fans of a warm, winter bowl of steaming porridge/ oatmeal can just tell that it's doing some good. Oats are one of the richest sources of beta-glucan, a soluble fibre excellent for digestion. Oats release sugar into the blood slowly (great for concentration!) and were used as an effective treatment for diabetes before insulin was invented.

FARRO

Another ancient variety of wheat, farro (also known as emmer) is similar to everyday wheat but is higher in protein, and especially in insoluble fibre, meaning it's great for digestion. It also contains less gluten than wheat, even more so if prepared properly. Its texture is a little like puffed rice and it was enjoyed by Italians for years before the superfood brigade caught on.

FREEKEH

Sounds like a 1970s disco band, but freekeh (also known as farik) is a wheat that is harvested while it's young and green, then roasted. A traditional food from the Middle East, because of the premature picking, it retains more protein, vitamins and minerals, and contains four times the fibre found in brown rice.

SCIENCE PHOTO LIBRARY, PICTUREPARTNERS © GETTY IMAGES

WHAT DO WE MEAN BY WHOLE GRAIN?

A whole grain is the best for you: it's any grain or cereal that consists of the bran (the outer layer of seed), the endosperm (the tissue inside the seed), and the cereal germ (the reproductive part of the seed that grows into a plant). This trifecta is usually separated when grains are refined and processed for commercial breakfast cereals, leaving little trace of any superfood power.

SPELT

Sweet, nutty spelt is an ancient grain (it even gets a mention in the Bible) that has risen in prominence relatively recently. It can be easier to digest than wheat, is rich in nutrients, and is particularly high in protein. It's an excellent source of manganese, copper and zinc. A loaf of home-made spelt bread (p64) may change your world.

IVAN BAJIC, WESTEND61 © GETTY IMAGES

GLUTEN-FREE GRAINS & CEREALS

For those with a gluten allergy or intolerance (particularly sufferers of coeliac disease), life can be tricky, mostly because gluten has a pesky habit of hiding in foods where one might not expect it, such as soups, tinned foods, even lipsticks (take care, gents). And while gluten sensitivity is increasing – perhaps due to the hybridisation of wheat – rest assured, gluten avoiders, that you are not immune from the superfood benefits of cereals and grains.

BROWN RICE

The most nutritious of the rices, brown rice is high in fibre, low on the glycaemic index, and brimming with natural vitamins and minerals, including zinc, copper, iron, manganese, selenium, Vitamin E, Vitamin B6, folate, thiamine and riboflavin to name but a few.

TEFF

Never heard of teff? It's new-ish on the superfood scene, though has been used in northeast African dishes for centuries. A native ingredient of Ethiopia, teff has a lovely nutty flavour and is a good source of protein, iron, manganese, thiamine, amino acids and Vitamin C.

BUCKWHEAT

There's more to buckwheat than pancakes (delicious though they are). High in fibre, it also contains all our essential amino acids, making it a complete protein. Buckwheat is particularly high in niacin, which is good for generating energy in the body.

PICTUREPARTNERS, BWFOLSOM, AMY_LV © GETTY IMAGES

DID INDIGENOUS AUSTRALIANS INVENT BREAD?

In his 2014 book, *Dark Emu, Black Seeds: Agriculture or Accident?*, author Bruce Pascoe contemplates the very real possibility that Indigenous Australians were the first to invent bread. Grindstones found at Cuddie Springs in northern New South Wales have been dated as being 30,000 years old: evidence that shows people were grinding seeds and grains 15,000 years before the ancient Egyptians used flour to make bread.

 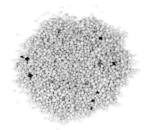 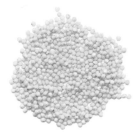

PICTUREPARTNERS, ROGER DIXON, FOTOLOTOS © GETTY IMAGES

QUINOA

A source of complete protein, quinoa contains every single amino acid we need, along with B vitamins, Vitamin E and fibre. It's heart-healthier than wheat, thanks to its monosaturated fats. Easily digested, quinoa has anti-inflammatory properties and is high in antioxidants.

AMARANTH

Meaning 'everlasting' in Greek, amaranth never completely softens when cooked (great for soups or porridges). It has more protein than oats and twice as much as white rice. Higher in healthy oils than other grains, amaranth helps to lower cholesterol. Good source of vitamins (A, C, E, K).

MILLET

It's thought that different varieties of millet were the staple food of Asia long before rice picked up the baton. High in protein, fibre and B vitamins, millet is light and easy to digest. High in magnesium and potassium, it also contributes to hearth health by helping to lower blood pressure.

YOU'LL NEED

½ cup **spelt flakes** (rolled spelt)

325mL (9 fl oz) water (warm in winter, cold in summer)

100g (3.5oz) seeds – **sunflower, linseed** or **pumpkin**, plus extra for rolling (optional)

2½ cups **ground spelt** – wholemeal or white

275mL (9 fl oz) water

1½ tsp salt

1 tsp fresh yeast, or ½ tsp dried yeast

1 tsp spices – aniseed or caraway (optional)

ORIGINS

The enduring popularity of *dinkelbrot* (literally spelt bread) stems in no small part from the fact that spelt, or *dinkel*, was the favoured grain of Hildegarde von Bingen, a medieval nun, composer, philosopher and natural scientist. A millennium later, she's still Germany's favourite health and wellbeing guru, and her oft-quoted guide to physical and spiritual vitality recommends eating spelt to promote everything from bigger muscles to a cheerful disposition.

FELBERT+EICKENBERG / STOCK4B, WESTEND61 © GETTY IMAGES

DINKELBROT

This traditional spelt-based loaf is the very essence of comfort, and embodies the German predilection for all things cosy, wholesome, earthy and nutritious.

METHOD

1 Place the spelt flakes and 50mL water in a bowl. Soak overnight. If you wish to add seeds to the bread, you can soak them separately in the same weight of water (ie 100g sunflower seeds in 100g water) overnight as well.

2 Put the soaked spelt flakes (and seeds, if using) and all the other ingredients in the mixing bowl of a food mixer and mix 15 minutes on slow, then 2 minutes on the second speed. If mixing by hand, knead until the dough comes off the side of the bowl (the dough should be smooth and lightly shiny on the surface).

3 Put the dough in a bowl and let it rest for 4–6 hours at room temperature (it's not essential but it makes the bread less dense if you fold or press down the dough an hour before shaping it).

4 Shape the dough into an oval ball. If you like, roll the dough in seeds or extra spelt flakes, then put it in a greased loaf pan.

5 Using a knife, slash the loaf down the centre. Sprinkle extra seeds on top. Again, let it rest for 1 hour at room temperature.

6 Place the loaf in the fridge and leave it to rest overnight for at least 12 hours, but no more than 20 hours.

7 Take the dough out of the fridge then preheat oven to 220°C (425°F)

8 Put the bread in the oven, reduce the temperature to 200ºC (400ºF) and bake it for 45–50 minutes. Remove from the oven and transfer to a wire cooling rack.

TASTING NOTES

A visit to any German supermarket reveals that the national standout food is bread, and the rich, earthy aromas wafting from the local bakery in every neighbourhood attest to the nation's expertise in all things bready. German breakfast is invariably comprised of fresh bread served on a wooden board with an array of toppings – butter, cheese, ham, and fruit preserves. Germans traditionally sat down to their main hot meal at lunchtime, but modern work life being what it is, they're now just as likely to tuck into an open sandwich served on *dinkelbrot*. Baked after minimal kneading, *dinkelbrot* has a firm, solid texture and nutty flavour enhanced by the toasted seeds that dot its dark honey-coloured crust. Best tasted with nothing more than a generous smear of butter. ● *by Sarah P Gilbert*

SOPHIE TURLEY © ALAMY

SERVES 8

YOU'LL NEED

2 cups stoneground **oatmeal**,
  plus extra for coating
½ tsp salt
¾ cup water
2 tbs butter

ORIGINS

Oats were the most common
grain grown in ancient Ireland
and, combined with some
butter, they could be baked
into a simple cracker-type cake
that made a good long-lasting
alternative to bread. Oatcakes
were taken into the fields by
labourers, on long journeys by
itinerant workers, and even
on transatlantic voyages. The
recipe has changed little
in centuries and the original
one remains the best.

IRELAND

DONEGAL OATCAKES

Coarse, dry oatcakes with their nutty flavour and crumbly texture are a cross between a cracker and a flatbread and taste delicious served with soft goat's cheese and smoked salmon.

METHOD

1 Put the oatmeal and salt into a bowl, mix them together and make a well in the centre.

2 Heat the water and butter in a pan until it is almost boiling.

3 Add the hot liquid to the dry ingredients.

4 Mix everything together with a wooden spoon to form a stiff dough.

5 Sprinkle the dough with a fine coating of oatmeal.

6 Roll out the dough thinly, about 5mm (¼in) thick, on a lightly floured surface.

7 Cut out circular shapes with a cookie cutter, before placing the rounds on a lightly greased baking sheet.

8 Cover the baking sheet with a clean dish towel and leave the rounds to dry out for about an hour.

9 Heat the oven to 200°C (400°F).

10 Bake the oatcakes for 20 minutes.

11 Turn over the oatcakes with a spatula – be careful as they can be quite fragile.

12 Cook the oatcakes for a further 10 minutes.

13 Remove the oatcakes from the oven.

14 Leave the oatcakes on the baking sheet for 2 minutes to firm up a little.

15 Transfer the oatcakes to a wire rack using a spatula and leave to cool. Oatcakes will keep in a sealed container for up to a week.

TASTING NOTES

Crunchy, nutty and oaty, light yet somehow substantial, oatcakes carry far more clout than a humble cracker. Oatcakes aren't something you'll find on a restaurant menu though; they're associated with a much more personal feast, ideally one enjoyed outdoors on the slopes of Mount Errigal, in the dunes on Marble Hill Beach, or while sitting in a bed of heather listening to the mournful whistle of golden plovers flying overhead as you relax after a hard morning of cutting turf on the bog. In such places there's something almost spiritual about eating oatcakes, knowing you are carrying on a tradition held dear to Donegal natives for centuries. ● *by Etain O'Carroll*

ORIGINS

A type of muesli was first devised in the 1900s for its health benefits by Swiss doctor Maximilian Bircher-Benner, after which the Bircher muesli dish is named. Bircher muesli is a 'wet' combination of oats and water, with chopped apples, nuts, lemon juice and cream, topped with honey. Modern recipes sometimes call for healthier yoghurt in place of the cream. In later years, muesli took on various drier guises. Today, it's a permanent breakfast fixture.

FOODCOLLECTION, JON ARNOLD © GETTY IMAGES

EUROPE (ESPECIALLY SWITZERLAND
AND GERMANY), USA, AUSTRALIA AND UK

MUESLI

Toasted or raw; three ingredients or 20; mushy or dry – infinitely
adaptable, muesli is simply one of the best choices for breakfast
or brunch and is packed with nutrition to boot.

YOU'LL NEED

3 cups **rolled oats**
1 cup **quinoa flakes**
½ cup **almonds**, chopped
½ cup **pumpkin seeds** (or
hemp seeds)
½ cup **walnuts**, chopped
1 cup sultanas
½ cup dried apricots, roughly
chopped
½ cup dried **coconut flakes**
(unsweetened)
½ cup **sunflower seeds**
½ cup **goji berries** or dried
cranberries
1 tbs ground cinnamon
dash of nutmeg
milk or yoghurt, to serve
fresh or stewed fruits, to
serve

METHOD

1 Place the oats in a large bowl.

2 Add the remaining ingredients, apart from the yoghurt
and fruit.

3 Mix everything thoroughly using your hands or a large spoon.

4 Store the mixture in an airtight container in a cupboard (not
in the refrigerator).

5 When you are ready to eat it, put a portion in a bowl and
serve with milk or yoghurt and top with fresh or stewed fruits.

TIP *The best thing about muesli? As well as being tantalising,
nutritious, and easy to make and serve, all experimentation is
good experimentation. Bircher muesli aside, there's no 'correct'
muesli recipe. This means you can try any combination of seeds
and nuts – and perfect it to meet your own needs. This recipe
is just one of many blends.*

TASTING NOTES

Tighten your dentures: it takes time to chomp through this nutty textured combination;
muesli belongs to the 'slow food' movement of another kind. But it's worth being unhurried,
as muesli is full of surprises: just as you're biting into an almond, there's a soft, juicy sultana
or, a coconut piece on the next chew. Don't skimp on quality yoghurts and accompaniments –
this can make or break the eating experience. Fresh, tangy berries (blueberries, blackberries,
raspberries and sliced strawberries) add moisture and acidity that counterbalance the dryness
and sweetness of the cereal, while banana provides a creamy, soft foil to the crunchy nuts.
Enjoy with a glass of freshly squeezed OJ and a thick newspaper. ● *by Kate Armstrong*

ORIGINS

It's thought that teff may have been cultivated as early as the first millennium BC by Pre-Aksumites in what is now northern Ethiopia, though there is no evidence of it being used to manufacture *injera* until the late 5th or 6th century AD. By the 13th century *injera* was a staple in the nation's diets, along with many of the dishes still popular in the country today. Early *injera* was baked on clay *mitads* (large clay discs) placed over an open flame.

TASTING NOTES

Slightly bitter and rubbery to the touch, *injera* never fails to make an impression. It usually arrives at your table in two guises: the first as a pancake filling your plate, on top of which are piled your chosen mains; the second, as a bit of a back-up, rolled up on a separate plate looking much like a hot towel on a plane. *Injera* is also the main instrument in dining, with patrons ripping off sections of it to use to grab portions of the dishes riding atop it, such as *doro wat* (chicken stew), *minchet abesh* (thick minced-meat stew topped with a boiled egg) and *kitfo* (warmed, but not cooked, minced beef with butter and spices). Its spongy nature is also great for soaking up leftover juices. ● *by Matt Phillips*

MAKES 5
INJERA

ETHIOPIA

INJERA

In Ethiopia *injera* isn't a mere dish, it's a pancake of countrywide proportions. Made with the native grain teff, *injera* is the base of almost every Ethiopian meal (and the key utensil too!).

YOU'LL NEED

¾ cups **teff**, ground
1 cup water
salt, to taste
¼ cup vegetable oil, for greasing the skillet
stews of your choice

METHOD

1 Mix the teff with the water in a bowl and let it stand at room temperature covered with a dish towel. Leave until it bubbles and has turned sour, which may take up to 3 days (occasionally overnight is enough time).

2 When the fermenting mixture has the consistency of a very thin pancake batter, stir in salt a pinch at a time until you can just start to detect its taste.

3 Lightly oil a 20cm (8in) or larger skillet and heat over a medium heat.

4 Pour just enough batter into the skillet to cover the bottom.

5 Cook briefly, until bubbles form and the edges start to lift from the pan. Hint: never flip the *injera*, and don't let it brown.

6 Remove from pan and allow to cool. Use foil or cling film wrap to avoid successive *injera* sticking together when stacking.

7 Serve with the stew of your choice.

LISA ROMEREIN/FOODPIX © GETTY IMAGES, GRANT ROONEY © ALAMY

ORIGINS

Quinoa cultivation dates back millennia in South America, but because the Spanish favoured cereal crops for sustenance after they arrived in the New World, a cloak of the unknown hung over this superfood until the late 20th century. This stew, however, embraces both indigenous and conquistador influences though – similar spicy quinoa dishes would have been consumed by the pre-Columbian civilisations, but without the Spanish-introduced garlic and tomato.

YOU'LL NEED

2 tbs **olive oil**
2 cups onions, peeled and chopped
1 cup celery, sliced
½ cup **carrots**, sliced
3 **garlic cloves**, peeled and minced
3 tsp ground cumin
1 tsp chilli powder
1 tsp ground coriander
a pinch cayenne pepper
2 tsp dried oregano
1 cup cooked **chickpeas**, rinsed
1 cup **green (bell) pepper**, diced
410g (14.5oz) can chopped **tomatoes** with juice
1 bay leaf
2 cups vegetable stock
410g (14.5oz) fresh **tomatoes**.
2 tsp fresh coriander leaves (cilantro), finely chopped
3 tbs **red wine vinegar**
½ cup **quinoa**
1 cup water

LAURI PATTERSON; BARTOSZ HADYNIAK © GETTY IMAGES

SERVES 4

QUINOA STEW

A feisty chilli, chickpea, and garlic-infused tomato stew laden to the gills with quinoa, this nutritious hearty hotpot has been warming the cockles of Andean folks since the dawn of time.

METHOD

1 Heat the oil in a large heavy-based pan. Saute the onions in oil for 5 minutes.

2 Add the celery and carrots and cook for 5 minutes more.

3 Add garlic and saute for a further 2 minutes.

4 Add the cumin, chilli powder, coriander, cayenne pepper and oregano and mix in well.

5 Add the chickpeas, green pepper, canned tomatoes, bay leaf and stock and bring to a boil.

6 Reduce the heat and simmer for 15 minutes, adding first the fresh tomatoes and then the fresh coriander (cilantro) and red wine vinegar towards the end of the cooking time.

7 As the stew is cooking, prepare the quinoa. Rinse the quinoa thoroughly, then add 1 cup water and cook over a medium heat, covered, for 15 minutes. Remove from the heat and set aside.

8 Serve by dividing the stew into bowls and add 2–3 heaped tablespoons of quinoa to each.

TASTING NOTES

Credit to the Andeans: few other regions of the world would bother to concoct what is first and foremost a belly-filler and devote so much attention to the seasoning. The simmered-soft quinoa (white quinoa is generally preferred by Peruvians and Bolivians) is the body of this dish but ideally you want to grab a spoonful with the tomato-doused chickpea-rich vegetable taste of the stew mixed in. The garlic, the herbs and the spice assail your senses a second later. To appreciate this dish to the maximum, try it on a bus-journey break in a middle-of-nowhere eatery high on the Andean plains. You'll walk in shivering, but after the old *abuela* (grandmother) has doled you out a bowl of this you'll feel heart-warmed. ● *by Luke Waterson*

ORIGINS

Alegría's principal ingredient, amaranth, served as one of the most important food sources for the Aztecs. It also played an important role in their religious ceremonies; Aztecs would create a statue of a celebrated god from amaranth and honey, and then divide it up for communion. The Spanish later outlawed amaranth due to its -association with indigenous religion. But the Aztecs' recipe endured and evolved into today's popular sweet.

YOU'LL NEED

½ cup unpopped **amaranth seeds**
½ cup **almonds**, or other nut of choice
1 cup *piloncillo* (Mexican cane sugar), or standard dark brown sugar
½ cup **honey**
½ tsp **lime juice**
½ cup dried fruit of choice, chopped

TASTING NOTES

Alegría can be found in Mexican markets and sweet shops that specialise in traditional and artisan candies; while it may seem a bit subdued when compared to colourful marzipan morsels or candied fruits sparkling with sugar, *alegría* finds perfection in its simplicity. The bars deliver a light, airy crunch, and the subtle flavours of the amaranth, almond and cane sugar play well with the bright zing of the dried fruit and the smooth sweetness of the honey. *Alegría* provides you with an eating experience that is both an historical legacy and a modern delight; plus, they are great fun to make! ● *by Bailey Johnson*

MARIASHUMOVA © GETTY IMAGES

MAKES 16
SMALL BARS

MEXICO

ALEGRÍA

These cheerful little bars – *alegría* means 'happiness' in Spanish – are a mainstay of Mexican snacking. Made mostly of honey and amaranth, these treats strike the perfect balance of sweet and earthy flavours.

METHOD

1 Heat a saucepan (no oil) over high heat; make sure to use a deep, heavy-bottomed pan, or the amaranth seeds will pop all over the kitchen!

2 Once the pan is very hot, drop about 1 tablespoon of amaranth into the pan and quickly cover. Remove the amaranth once all the seeds have popped, and repeat until all the amaranth has been used. Pro tip: if the amaranth doesn't immediately start to pop, the pan isn't hot enough and the seeds will cook unevenly and burn quickly. It's handy to have a little extra amaranth on hand, just in case.

3 Lightly toast the almonds in the same dry pan until they are browned and crispy.

4 Combine the *piloncillo*, honey and lime juice in a pan over a medium heat, stirring to combine.

5 Bring the mixture to the boil, and allow it to boil for seven to ten minutes, or until the mixture has thickened.

6 Combine popped amaranth and the sugar and honey mixture in a large bowl.

7 Line a large baking sheet with parchment paper, then spread the almonds and dried fruit across the surface. Add the amaranth mixture, patting it flat into the pan. Pro tip: since the mixture will be hot, use another sheet of parchment paper to press it down evenly. Make sure it is compact, so the bars don't fall apart later.

8 Leave it to cool for half an hour, then cut into squares. Store in an airtight container for up to 5 days.

TONY ANDERSON © GETTY IMAGES

MATILDA DELVES © GETTY IMAGES

FRUITS

Sure, all fruit is good for you, but what takes it to the next level? What makes a superfruit? We're talking about fruits that are so packed with antioxidants and nutrients that regular consumption will help you live longer, make your skin and hair shine, and give your body the best chance of fighting off disease. Juice bars have been big business over the past decade (notably the cold-pressed juice movement), and while some fruit juice is better than none, the high amount of calories and natural sugars (along with minimal fibre) consumed in a drink outweigh the portable benefits. Wherever possible, eat your superfruit, don't drink it. →

HISTORY

Various fruits were first cultivated at different times. Between 6000 and 3000 BC Mediterranean fruit, such as dates, olives, grapes, figs and pomegranates, came to prominence. Citrus fruits, stone fruits, and various pomes (ie apples, pears) were harvested in Central and East Asia, and also in Western cultures. Other fruits, such as lingonberries and durian, though widely known, are relatively new. It's also worth noting that the geographic origin of a fruit is not necessarily obvious from its present-day associations.

HEALTH BENEFITS

For maximum health benefits, all fruit needs to be eaten as fresh as possible. Tinned fruit in 'natural' juices, processed fruit, crazy-coloured fruit lollies, fruit flattened, rolled, preserved and packaged into strips or bars: no. Step away from those things. If you can't eat your fruit freshly picked from the source, frozen is regarded as being the next best thing. The key is eating fruit in its whole state (skin and all) as this is where the nutrient action is. Tomatoes (p80) are the only fruits that are actually better for you when cooked, rather than eaten in their raw form.

MORSA IMAGES, JOHNER IMAGES © GETTY IMAGES

DID YOU KNOW?

For more than 200 years, tomatoes were thought to be poisonous and certainly not a ubiquitous part of Italian pasta dishes! In the 1700s, Europeans were wary of the tomato's bright colour and suspected it was killing aristocrats. In fact, it was the high lead content of the pewter plates that was to blame.

VARIANTS

Can't decide on your favourite fruit? Then a fruit hybrid might cover all your needs. A tangelo, which looks a bit like a bumpy orange, is a delicious citrus hybrid of tangerine and pomelo or grapefruit. The unsavourily named ugli fruit is the Jamaican variety of a tangelo: a blend of tangerine, grapefruit and Seville orange. How about a mixture of raspberries, loganberries and blackberries? That's called a boysenberry. Can't decide between a plum or an apricot? You don't have to: there's a pluot for that; more plum than apricot, they have a tart flavour and are great in salads. All of this is not some freaky genetic modification but rather, a result of natural cross-pollination – swapping pollen from one fruit flower to another.

BERRIES

The word 'berry' is probably the most frequently mentioned when it comes to superfoods. And for good reason. Whether it's the resveratrol, a powerful phytonutrient present mostly in grape skins that is linked to longevity, or the antioxidants in blueberries, which are an easy fruit to add to cereal or to pack in a picnic. And yes, grapes are, botanically, considered berries: the true definition being that the entire fruit wall is fleshy. If you're surprised that a tomato is a fruit (it has seeds, so yes), then you'll be further surprised to learn it also fits the berry definition.

TOMATOES

It is best to cook tomatoes in order to increase the lycopene, which is an antioxidant thought to reduce the risk of heart disease and cancer and improve bone health. While heating does decrease Vitamin C levels, the trade-off is worth it.

GOJI BERRIES

Unusually good for your eyes, goji berries contain a powerful antioxidant, zeaxanthin, which absorbs blue light to protect your retinas. This decreases the risk of age-related macular degeneration, the main cause of blindness in the elderly.

GRAPES

Revered since ancient times, grapes have excellent anti-inflammatory properties and a low glycaemic index. Studies have also linked them to prevention of some cancers. Remember: the darker the grape skin, the higher the antioxidant content.

FLOORTJE, C SQUARED STUDIOS © GETTY IMAGES

SUPERFRUITS & SUPERFOODS

Be cautious when it comes to 'superfruit' marketing. It's a term that's been used fairly loosely in the food and beverage industry since 2004. Unlike 'superfoods', which has some strict criteria in the European Union (namely, since 2007, a product can't be marketed in the EU as a superfood unless credible scientific research backs it up), any product manufacturer can call anything a superfruit.

BLUEBERRIES

The aptly named blueberries contain plenty of manganese (a mineral that gives you energy), Vitamin C and Vitamin K (good for bone health), as well as fibre. They are also thought to help protect against heart disease, cancer and diabetes.

AÇAÍ BERRIES

Some believe these berries fight the effects of anti-ageing more than other fruits, others suggest this occurrence happens only as part of a balanced diet. Either way, there's no denying açaí berries are loaded with antioxidants and nutrients.

CLOUDBERRIES

Hello Nordic superfood: cloudberries hail all the way from Lapland and, as they are difficult to source, are rather expensive. They are very rich in vitamins and their leaves are used as a medicinal herb. Worth a foodie trip to Scandinavia then.

CREATIVEYE99/ LEW ROBERTSON/ MAXSOL2 © GETTY IMAGES

OTHER SUPERFRUITS

OLIVES

With high levels of monounsaturated fats (good for heart health), olives are also rich in Vitamin E, antioxidants and polyphenols to boost the immune system, as well as being a source of protein. Extra virgin olive oil is also a popular by-product.

KAKADU PLUMS

A fruit native to northwestern Australia, Kakadu plums (also known as gubinge) are commonly used in jams, pickles and chutneys. Loaded with antioxidants, Vitamin C, Vitamin E, as well as zinc, calcium, magnesium and folate, they're worth eating.

AVOCADOS

They're everywhere smashed on toast (p112) at hip brunch spots! High in healthy monosaturated fats (like olives) they help lower cholesterol and protect your body from heart disease, as well as degenerative eye and brain diseases.

REDHELGA, SUBJUG © GETTY IMAGES, DAVID HANCOCK © ALAMY

BON APPETIT © ALAMY, BRUNO CRESCIA PHOTOGRAPHY INC; LOVE_LIFE © GETTY IMAGES

WHICH OLIVES ARE HEALTHIEST?

Take care with your sodium intake when eating olives, as large amounts of salt are usually added during the preserving process. (Sadly, unpreserved is not really an option: eating an olive straight from the tree is a very bitter experience indeed!) Black olives have less saturated fat and are best for boosting your iron levels, while green olives contain twice as much Vitamin E as black olives, which helps prevent cell damage.

QUANDONGS

The quandong is a native peach that is not new to indigenous Australians, but superchef René Redzepi gave it international attention on the menu at his 2016 Noma pop-up in Sydney. With twice the Vitamin C of an orange, it's a rich source of antioxidants.

POMEGRANATES

Gleaming red pomegranate seeds add a big dose of antioxidants (thought to contain more than a cup of green tea) to any dish. They may slow the growth of prostate cancer, reduce dental plaque and help prevent osteoporosis.

DATES

These Middle Eastern soft fruits are an excellent source of energy, have higher antioxidant levels than other dried fruits and are full of easily digested vitamins and minerals. With lots of fibre, they are also great for bowel health.

ORIGINS

The berries of the Amazonian açaí palm were barely known outside the Amazon until the 1970s. In the following decade the legendary Brazilian ju-jitsu founder Carlos Gracie popularised açaí bowl in Rio de Janeiro, and it wasn't long before local surfers adopted the snack as the perfect post-session pick-me-up. In the early noughties, the first batch of açaí pulp winged its way to the USA, and Hawaii and Southern California became the first places where açaí bowl found a foreign home. It's now found from Sydney to London.

YOU'LL NEED

2 heaped tbs freeze-dried açaí powder or about 110g (4oz) slightly thawed açaí pulp

2 heaped tbs milled seeds (chia, flax, sunflower etc)

⅔ cup almond milk, coconut milk, coconut water, or apple juice

1½ cups frozen blueberries and/or sliced banana

For the toppings

⅔ cup fresh seasonal berries and/or figs

1 ripe banana, sliced

4 tbs muesli or oats

2 tbs seeds or other toppings (try flaxseed, chia seeds, shredded coconut, jungle peanuts and/or bee pollen)

SAMBAPHOTO/ROGERIO ASSIS © GETTY IMAGES

BRAZIL

AÇAÍ BOWL

It looks like ice cream, and tastes like ice cream, but this tropical Brazilian superfood snack couldn't be healthier. Refreshingly cool and satisfyingly filling, it's heaven in a bowl.

METHOD

1 Blend the açaí powder/pulp with the milled seeds, liquid and frozen fruit.

2 Add more liquid until it reaches the desired consistency, according to your personal taste.

3 Transfer the mixture to a breakfast bowl and serve immediately.

4 Top the mixture with fresh berries and/or figs, sliced banana, muesli (or oats) and seeds, in whichever combination you prefer.

TIP *Choose the liquid to blend with the açaí powder/pulp to suit your personal taste; the milkier the liquid, the creamier the mixture will be.*

TASTING NOTES

Waking up on a hot, sticky morning by the Brazilian seaside, the cool combination of berries and nuts in an açaí bowl provide the ultimate wake-up call, with a health kick to boot. With a similar consistency to lightly-defrosted gelato, the rich, deep-purple açaí pulp or powder mixture forms the basis of this attractive tropical dish. Traditional Brazilian toppings include sliced banana and a sprinkling of granola, but Western cafes usually also offer an additional range of healthy toppings such as blueberries, shaved coconut, seeds and nuts. While the açaí mixture, which tastes a little bit like blackberries mixed with dark chocolate, is deliciously moreish by itself, the crunch of nuts provides delightful texture. ● *by Sarah Reid*

MARCELOKRELLING © GETTY IMAGES

ORIGINS

Andalusians credit the invention of gazpacho to the Romans, though obviously the Roman version came a few centuries too early to include tomatoes. This proto-gazpacho was most likely conceived as a way to use up stale bread in peasant kitchens, consisting of little more than old crusts, vinegar, water, olive oil and salt. In time, the Romans left and Cordoba and Seville became the de facto home of gazpacho, spawning a host of vegetable variations.

TASTING NOTES

The funny thing about cold soup is that it needs to be eaten when it's hot – about 35°C (95°F) in the shade would do it, ideally on the terrace of an Andalusian villa. Against this baking backdrop, the unlikely combination of stale bread, garlic, olive oil, wine vinegar and fresh-from-the-garden vegetables, pounded together and chilled, is deliciously refreshing. This is the sun-kissed taste of the Mediterranean countryside in a savoury smoothie. Variations abound. In Cádiz, sparse water supplies led to the creation of *arranque roteño*, so thick it could almost be a dip. In Extremadura, hunks of ham are added to the mix. To be truly authentic, any gazpacho should be pounded with a pestle and mortar to release the flavours. ● *by Joe Bindloss*

BRIAN HAGIWARA, MORSA IMAGES © GETTY IMAGES

SERVES 4

SPAIN

GAZPACHO

Like revenge, gazpacho is a dish best served cold; its icy medley of pounded vegetables, vinegar, olive oil and leftover bread is the perfect antidote to the Mediterranean heat.

YOU'LL NEED

2 garlic cloves, peeled and diced

1 red onion, peeled and diced

1 red (bell) pepper, deseeded and diced

½ cucumber, diced

500g (17oz) ripe plum (roma) tomatoes, diced

100g (3.5oz) stale crusty white bread, broken into small chunks

salt and ground black pepper, to taste

4 tbs olive oil, plus extra for brushing toast

1 cup passata

4 tbs sherry vinegar

1 tsp sugar

toasted crusty white bread, to serve

METHOD

1 Place diced garlic, onion, pepper, cucumber and tomatoes together in a large bowl.

2 Add the bread and season with salt and pepper, to taste.

3 Add the olive oil, passata, sherry vinegar and sugar.

4 Squeeze the mixture together with your hands to blend the flavours.

5 Cover and place in the fridge overnight to chill.

6 Remove from the fridge and pound the mixture in a pestle and mortar, to make a smooth mix (alternatively, blend in a food processor).

7 Return to the fridge until ready to serve.

8 Present your gazpacho at the table, served with toasted crusty white bread, brushed with olive oil and seasoned with salt and pepper, for dipping.

ORIGINS

People have been cultivating millet in northern China for more than 6000 years, and the goji berry – used to ward off back pain, dizziness and eyesight problems – has been part of traditional Chinese medicine for almost as long. Exactly when some bright spark decided to put them together is unclear, but it seems that the Chinese have been using goji goodness to jazz up their porridge for as long as anyone north of the Yangtze can remember.

SERVES 4

GOJI BERRY MILLET PORRIDGE

Served on breakfast tables across China for centuries, this simple, warming, congee-like porridge combines the nutty flavours of millet with a sprinkling of superfood fruitiness from the nutrition-packed goji berry.

YOU'LL NEED

1.5L (6 cups) water
5 tbs **millet**, rinsed
2 tbs dried **goji berries**, rinsed
sesame-seed buns (*shāobing*)

METHOD

1 Place the water in a large pan and bring to the boil.

2 Add the millet and reduce the heat to a simmer.

3 Stir from time to time.

4 After 15 minutes, add the goji berries.

5 After a further 15 minutes, or when the porridge has reached your preferred consistency, take the pan off the heat.

6 Stir one final time, then serve, preferably with freshly baked sesame-seed buns (*shāobing*).

TASTING NOTES

Cheap, abundant and fabulously filling, millet porridge is the breakfast staple of choice for much of northern China so you're just as likely to find it in well-to-do family homes as you are on the plastic fold-out tables of pop-up, street-side breakfast restaurants, tucked away down the back alleys of old Beijing. It isn't always served with goji berries, but when it is, it's a treat. Millet porridge has a subtle nuttiness, but to the uninitiated it can seem slightly bland. Adding goji berries not only ramps up the health benefits up a notch, but also adds some raisin-like texture and a pinch of natural sweetness to every mouthful. For the perfect dip-and-slurp breakfast combo, serve it with freshly baked sesame-seed buns, known in China as *shāobing*. ● *by Daniel McCrohan*

PILIPPHOTO © GETTY IMAGES

JUSTIN FOULKES © LONELY PLANET

ORIGINS

Greeks have been making must cake, also known as *moustopita* or *petimezopita*, since before anyone can remember. Its special ingredient, *petimezi*, the world's oldest natural sweetener, harks back to ancient Greek times. Hippocrates (he of 'let food be thy medicine' fame), refers to its energy-giving power as far back as the 5th century BC. The ancient Romans also had a version of must cake called *mustaceum*, traditionally eaten as a digestif after heavy meals.

YOU'LL NEED

knob of butter, for greasing
400g (14oz) self-raising flour
1 tsp cream of tartar
1½ tsp bicarb soda (baking powder)
½ tsp ground cloves
1 tbs ground cinnamon
50g (2oz) walnuts, chopped
80g (3oz) currants
80g (3oz) raisins
zest of 1 large orange
1 cup petimezi (concentrated grape syrup)
1 cup olive oil
1 cup orange juice (preferably freshly squeezed)
1 tbs red wine vinegar
100g (3½oz) caster sugar
4 tbs brandy (or Greek *tsipouro*, ouzo or *rakı*, according to your personal preference)

TASTING NOTES

It's September, the harsh Greek sun is setting and the last of the grapes have been harvested. Let the singing and dancing commence! Amid the flurry of hands clapping and swerving around circles of revellers dancing, a friendly local slaps you on the back and hands over a glass of wine and a wedge of what looks like a dark, moist carrot cake. '*Kali orexi*!'. The cake's aroma is intoxicating, the fug of its heady, sweet richness inviting a rushed taste. With the first bite comes a little crunch of walnut, along with familiarity and happy confusion: the cloves and cinnamon are reminiscent of gingerbread, yet the juicy raisins and currants change your mind again. As the lingering smell of orange and fermented grapes further intrigues, perhaps a second helping might shed more light. You'll dance later. ● by Karyn Noble

GREECE

MUST CAKE

MAKES
A 25CM
DIAMETER
CAKE

A cake made especially to celebrate a successful wine harvest? That sounds like Greece. This fruit-and-walnut-laden speciality has a superfood secret weapon: *petimezi*, a molasses-like syrup slowly simmered from the must of grapes.

METHOD

1 Preheat your oven to 180°C (350°F) and lightly grease a 25cm (10in) cake tin with a knob of butter (or vegans, use olive oil).

2 In a large bowl, sift together the flour, cream of tartar, bicarb soda, cloves and cinnamon.

3 In a separate bowl, combine the chopped walnuts, currants, raisins and orange zest.

4 Stir in 2 tablespoons of the flour mixture from step 2 and combine well to make a sweet dried-fruit mixture.

5 Pour the petimezi, olive oil, orange juice, vinegar and sugar into a liquidiser or food processer and blend for approximately 4 minutes, until smooth and emulsified.

6 Pour the liquid mixture into the bowl of dry ingredients from step 2, and mix this together into a smooth batter.

7 Get your dried fruit mixture from step 3 and stir this into the cake batter.

8 Pour the cake batter into your greased cake tin and bake for 50 minutes in the preheated oven.

9 Remove the cake from the oven. Test if it's ready by inserting a skewer – if it comes out clean, you're good to go.

10 Let it sit in the tin to settle for 5 minutes. Yes, it smells spectacular, but try not to taste yet.

11 Turn the cake on to a plate or serving dish and sprinkle with brandy or your traditional Greek spirit of choice. Cut into generous portions and serve.

IMAGEBROKER © ALAMY

ORIGINS

Horiatiki in Greek translates to 'peasant salad', so it's safe to assume the origins are rural in nature. The salad's essential ingredients are believed to be what farmers would bring to the fields for their snack, though it's thought they would keep the constituents whole and bite straight into each item separately. This eventually evolved into the mixed salad we see today, complete with a sprinkling of oregano and dollop of olive oil and vinegar.

SAM STOWELL; THANASIS ZOVOILIS © GETTY IMAGES

SERVES 4

HORIATIKI (GREEK SALAD)

The Greek salad has plenty of pretenders, but the original is the *horiatiki*. As simple as it is full of fresh flavours, it screams of the Mediterranean and summer.

YOU'LL NEED

150g (5oz) Greek feta
2 green (bell) peppers, deseeded and roughly chopped
1 large cucumber, peeled and roughly chopped
1 small red onion, peeled and diced
5 ripe tomatoes, roughly chopped
350g (12oz) Kalamata olives, pitted
1 tsp dried oregano
3–4 tbs extra virgin olive oil
3–4 tbs red wine vinegar

METHOD

1 Place the chopped ingredients in a large bowl with the olives.

2 Crumble the feta over the mixture, followed by a sprinkling of oregano, olive oil and red wine vinegar.

3 Mix well and serve.

TASTING NOTES

The summer sun is shining down and you're having a lazy lunch in a Greek taverna by the sea (preferably with your toes in the sand). The coolness of *horiatiki* cuts through the heat, and the variety of tastes in it blend brilliantly: the sweetness of the tomatoes, the slight bitterness of the green peppers, the saltiness of the feta, the sharpness of the red onion and cleansing nature of the cucumber. ● *by Matt Phillips*

YOU'LL NEED

350g (12oz) *juustoleipä*
  cheese (if unavailable, try
  Pasture Pride juusto cheese)
15–25 **cloudberries**, fresh OR
  5 tbs **cloudberry jam**
muscovado sugar, to taste
5 tbs double cream

ORIGINS

Foraging for berries is so
enshrined into Finnish culture
there are even laws about it. The
cloudberry might be a sought-after superfood worldwide
today, but monks at Nådendal
Abbey (southwest Finland) were
extolling the health benefits as
long ago as the Middle Ages.
Lapland is the country's proud
cloudberry cradle but Southern
Ostrobothnia and Kainuu regions
vie with the Laplanders over who
invented *juustoleipä*. Baking
fruit and cheese together with
cream, we assume, was first done
somewhere in-between...

RAINBOW33 © ALAMY, ANNAILEYSH © GETTY IMAGES

SERVES 4

BAKED JUUSTOLEIPÄ WITH CLOUDBERRIES

Among Finland's 50-odd wild berry species, the cloudberry is the Holy Grail: known as 'Lapland's Gold' because of its elusiveness. Baked with *juustoleipä* cheese, it is the nation's unique (and downright yummy) dessert.

METHOD

1 Cut the *juustoleipä* into 1–2cm (½in) squares and spread evenly across the bottom of a lightly greased baking dish.

2 Scatter a quarter of the fresh cloudberries OR spread 1–2 tbs of the cloudberry jam over the squares of *juustoleipä*.

3 Sprinkle a little muscovado sugar over the *juustoleipä* and cloudberry mixture. This should not be too much, but just sufficient to counterbalance the tartness of the cloudberries.

4 Pour over the double cream. The *juustoleipä* and cloudberry mixture should be partially but not totally covered.

5 Place the dish under the grill and cook under a medium heat until the sugar has caramelised and the top looks golden-brown.

6 Serve with the remaining cloudberries.

TASTING NOTES

Juustoleipä was always a foodstuff designed to endure. A fresh, mild cheese made from cow's milk or, in the north, reindeer's milk, its purpose was not to please palates but to fill boots and, when dried, lasted years: ideal for the poor in isolated Finnish communities. The tradition of baking *juustoleipä* began because this softened the age-hardened cheese for ease of eating. Now, the trademark golden-brown burnished outer blotches (as if from the hot hearthstones of old) and 'squeak' as your teeth clamp down are what Finns demand from their baked *juustoleipä*. The taste shoots in from the cloudberries (tart, with a gooseberry-ish tang) and the double cream and muscovado sugar sauce. Lapland still has plenty of traditional Finnish restaurants serving the dessert. Here the cloudberries are freshest – probably hand-plucked from a forest near your table. ● *by Luke Waterson*

ORIGINS

This concoction unites thousands of years of history. Red
dates have been eaten in China
for over 8000 years. Ginseng
has been prized for millenia as
beneficial to health – even the
name 'ginseng' means 'person
root'. Goji berries have also
fuelled Chinese history for well
over 2000 years. Legend has
it that people observed that
residents who lived near wells in
which goji berries dropped lived
to be over 100 years old.
The soup's name refers to the
Silkie, a fluffy chicken with
dark skin.

SERVES 4–6

CHINA

BAMBOO SILKIE SOUP

The goji berry joins forces with herbaceous ginseng and sweet Chinese red dates to form a chicken soup supergroup with an impressive depth of flavour.

YOU'LL NEED

1 chicken (Silkie or small-size), cut into small pieces (ask your butcher to do this)
1 cup dried red dates, rinsed
½ cup dried goji berries, rinsed
3 stems of ginseng
2 tsp salt

METHOD

1 Place the chicken pieces in a pan with enough water to cover and boil for 10 minutes.

2 Remove the chicken and discard the water.

3 Place the chicken and the rest of the ingredients in a large pan with fresh water to cover and bring to the boil.

4 Reduce the heat and simmer for 1 hour or until the chicken is tender and fully cooked.

5 Serve hot in individual bowls.

TASTING NOTES

You've spent the afternoon wandering the town and now head to a *hútòng* (narrow alleyway) with your guide, where the city noise fades as you enter a family courtyard to your dinner invitation. You lift the porcelain lid of your bowl and before you even taste the soup, the herbal fragrance of ginseng and chicken mixes with the scent of charcoal from the old stove. You huddle close for the first ladleful and the hot broth brings a rush of warmth. The woody sweetness of the ginseng and fleshy dates lingers on the lips. At first the taste seems thin, but the bursts of goji berries and the perfume of chicken shine through and keeps you scooping up more. If you can't get your hands on ginseng, ginger is an excellent, punchy alternative. ● *by Philip Tang*

TOP PHOTO CORP © STOCKFOOD

YOU'LL NEED

4 tbs palm sugar
3 tbs fish sauce
2 tbs tamarind concentrate
4 tbs lime juice
4 **garlic cloves**, peeled
salt
4 bird's eye chillies
3 tbs roasted peanuts
3 tbs dried prawns, rinsed and
  dried
8 **cherry tomatoes**, quartered
4 **snake beans**, chopped
3 cups **green papaya**,
  shredded

ORIGINS

Som tam most likely has its
origins in neighbouring Laos,
where it's known as *tam maak
hung* and is a culinary staple.
Residents of northeast Thailand,
who have many cultural and culinary links with Laos, probably
introduced the dish to the rest
of Thailand during their stints
as migrant labourers as early
as the 1950s. It didn't take long
to catch on, and *som tam* can
now be found in virtually every
corner of the country.

TIM BEWER, AUSTIN BUSH © GETTY IMAGES

SERVES 4

SOM TAM

Spicy, tart, crunchy, salty and sweet – five reasons why *som tam*, an often ballistically-spicy green-papaya 'salad' that combines them all, is quite possibly Thailand's best-loved street-food dish.

METHOD

1 Make the dressing by mixing the palm sugar, fish sauce, tamarind concentrate and 3 tbs of the lime juice.

2 Using a large mortar and pestle, crush the garlic with some salt, then add the bird's eye chillies, roasted peanuts, dried prawns and the rest of the lime juice and pound until it resembles a coarse paste.

3 Add the cherry tomatoes and snake beans and lightly bruise (but do not crush) with the paste.

4 Put the green papaya in a large salad bowl, stir in the paste and the dressing and gently toss with a large spoon.

5 Serve as a side dish in a Thai banquet or with steamed rice and raw vegetables such as cabbage and green beans.

TIP *Try to make this salad a couple of hours before serving so that the papaya can absorb all the flavours.*

TASTING NOTES

Although now served in some restaurants, *som tam* is still associated with the street stalls run by residents of northeast Thailand. As is often the case with Thai-style street food, ordering *som tam* requires advance discussion, with diners telling the woman operating the mortar and pestle how many chillies or how much sugar they prefer. Thais from northeastern Thailand tend to prefer 'Lao'-style *som tam*, which contains *plaa raa* (unpasteurised fermented fish sauce) and chunks of eggplant. Most others go for 'Thai' *som tam*, which is sweeter, containing peanuts and dried shrimp and seasoned with bottled fish sauce. Either way, the application of chilli and lime juice provide the defining flavours of *som tam*: spicy and tart. ● *by Austin Bush*

ORIGINS

For millennia the quandong has been a superfood for Indigenous Australians such as the Pitjantjatjara, who live in the unforgiving Central Desert. High in vitamins and rudely resplendent in flavour, the fruit is used in savoury and sweet dishes, and its roots are employed in traditional medicine. European settlers quickly embraced the quandong, and soon the wild peach was tamed inside jam jars and tasty pastry prisons, typically liberated after Sunday dinner.

YOU'LL NEED

1 cup quandongs, pitted (use frozen, fresh or dried, but if the latter, soak overnight)
1 cup water
½ tsp lemon juice
½ cup white sugar
1 apple, peeled, cored and thinly sliced (sweet rather than a tart apple)
1 tbs cornflour
a dash of water
2 sheets of shortcrust pastry (ready-made pie-crust pastry)
1 egg, beaten
¼ tsp native Australian fruit dukkah (or ground cinnamon)

NOTE *The dukkah is made from dried quandong, shaved finger lime, and various native nuts, but may vary.*

BON APPETIT © ALAMY

MAKES A 20CM DIAMETER PIE

OUTBACK, AUSTRALIA

QUANDONG PIE

Indigenous bush-tucker knowledge and traditional Western home-baking skills collide to create this fusion feast, which wraps the finest fruit of the Australian desert – the native peach – in a sweet settler-style pastry.

METHOD

1 Combine the quandongs, water, lemon juice and sugar in a pan, bring to the boil and simmer until it's quite thick, then add the apple.

2 Make a paste with the cornflour (add a dash of water) and stir this into the simmering sauce.

3 When the mixture begins to bubble, remove from the heat and let it cool.

4 Grease a 20cm (8in) pie tin and line it with pastry, making sure it's pressed well into the sides and that any seams are overlapped.

5 Pour the cooled quandong mix into the pie dish, until it's about 75 per cent full.

6 Brush the edge of the pie crust with the beaten egg and add a pastry lid.

7 Pattern the pie as you please with a fork, poke a few breathing holes in the top, brush with more egg and dust your creation with a pinch of sugar and the dukkah (or cinnamon).

8 Place the pie on the middle shelf of the oven and bake at 180°C (350°F) for 30–45 minutes, or until the pastry has a pleasing Aussie tan.

TIP *For a vegan version, be sure to use vegan pastry, canola oil for greasing the pie tin and a light olive oil to replace the egg wash.*

TASTING NOTES

Moisture is at a premium in the arid Aussie Outback, where sinking your jaws into a juicy quandong is quite the sensational experience, whether you're ruminating on them raw or face-diving a freshly baked pie straight from the camp oven. If you're rustling up this recipe at home in the civilised embrace of a modern kitchen, the fragrant ingredients will introduce a bit of bona fide bush ambience to your otherwise urban surrounds. As the cooking quandongs caramelise, throw the windows open and let the wonderful whiff of the wild peach reach out and conjure up the call of kookaburras and cockatoos, real or imagined. ● *by Patrick Kinsella*

ORIGINS

The caper plant is thought to have been imported to the south of France by the Phocaeans, who hailed from an Ionian Greek city on the western Anatolian coast and settled near Marseilles in the 6th century BC. The plant's flowering buds, known as *tapeno*, were preserved in olive oil in amphora. In the process, the buds were crushed to form a tasty paste. This was the basis of the dish known today as tapenade. Down the ages other ingredients, such as crushed black olives, have been added.

MATTEO COLOMBO; NORMAN HOLLANDS © GETTY IMAGES

SERVES 4

FRANCE

TAPENADE

The ideal accompaniment for a chilled glass of wine, this *umami*-rich Provençal dip is named after the local lingo for capers, even though black olives are the principal ingredient.

YOU'LL NEED

200g (7oz) whole black olives
3 tbs capers
2 anchovy fillets
2 tsp fresh thyme
1 fat garlic clove
2–3 tsp lemon juice
5 tbs extra virgin olive oil
sprinkle of ground black
   pepper

METHOD

1 Remove the pits from the olives.

2 Roughly chop the capers, anchovy fillets and thyme, and crush the garlic.

3 Add the olives, capers, anchovies, thyme and garlic to a food processor and blend to a rough paste.

4 Add the lemon juice and whizz into the paste.

5 With the motor still running, add in the oil.

6 Season with pepper and more lemon juice to taste.

TIP *If using a pestle and mortar rather than a food processor, crush the garlic, anchovies, capers and thyme together first, later adding the olives. Then add the oil and lemon juice gradually, pounding the mixture between pours.*

TASTING NOTES

Packed with punchy flavours, tapenade conjures up balmy days spent under the Mediterranean sun. The key ingredients are earthy black olives and tart capers. Use whole olives rather than ready-pitted sort, as they will taste better, and preferably either Niçoise or Kalamata varieties. Capers packed in salt will also provide a superior taste but if you go this way make sure you rinse the buds well before use. A couple of anchovies adds a salty undertone to the purple-and-green flecked paste, while a little garlic makes the recipe unmistakably Gallic. A generous dash of lemon juice and fragrant thyme provide sparkling acidity and a fresh herbiness to the mix. Load a generous amount on to a cracker or thin slice of baguette and you have the perfect appetiser. ● *by Simon Richmond*

ORIGINS

The Aztecs were thought to have first whipped up a batch of guacamole between the 14th and 16th centuries. It was originally considered a sauce, deriving its name from the Aztec words 'ahuacatl' meaning avocado and 'mulli' meaning sauce. As most of their diet was relatively low in fat, the Aztecs relied on the buttery goodness of guacamole. When the Spanish invaded Mexico in the 1500s, they found the Aztecs using traditional 'molcajetes' (basalt pestle and mortars) to mash up avocados.

MAKES 4~6 SERVINGS

MEXICO

GUACAMOLE

Mexico's tangy green dip sees the smooth silkiness of mashed avocados cleverly enlivened with zinging lemon or lime, chilli or cayenne pepper, jalapeño, onion and garlic. Guaranteed to break the ice at any fiesta.

YOU'LL NEED

½ red onion, peeled and finely chopped
1 serrano chilli, finely chopped
1–2 tsp sea salt
3 ripe **Hass avocados**, skinned and destoned
2 limes
handful of fresh coriander leaves (cilantro), chopped
1–2 ripe medium-sized **tomatoes**, deseeded and chopped
ground black pepper, to taste

METHOD

1 Place a quarter of the red onion, half the chilli, and the salt into a pestle and mortar and mash until it forms to a rough paste.

2 Place the avocado flesh into the pestle and mortar.

3 Use a fork to mash the flesh into the mixture, adding half the lime juice little by little.

4 Add the rest of the chilli and lime juice, red onion, coriander and tomato.

5 Season with black pepper.

6 Taste and adjust the flavour with more salt, lime or coriander, depending upon your preference.

TASTING NOTES

Best enjoyed at its freshest, guacamole should be served straight from the *molcajete*. While much of the globe scoops it dollop by dollop straight from the tub to their mouths using tortilla chips, the more authentic way to enjoy it is by smearing it on a taco as a crucial part of the Mexican condiment trio: guacamole, salsa and sour cream. Like the country itself, every mouthful exudes colour and character, being at once fiery and velvety; crunchy and smooth, and delivering a rush of pepper here, a fresh morsel of tomato or a burst of onion there. ● *by Helen Brown*

CLAUDIA TOTIR: NICOLEBRANAN @ GETTY IMAGES. JUSTIN FOULKES @ LONELY PLANET

YOU'LL NEED

75g (½ cup) walnuts, cut into
  quarters
500g (2 cups) pitted dates
200g (7oz) unsalted butter
4 tbs caster sugar
1½ cups plain (all-purpose)
  flour
¼ tsp ground cardamom
½ tsp ground cinnamon
2 tbs ground pistachios
1 tbs desiccated coconut
  (optional)

ORIGINS

The stifling heat of summer in
Iran may make day-to-day activi-
ties a chore – but it's the perfect
breeding ground for date palms,
which thrive along the Persian
Gulf. The country produces a glut
of these sticky, sweet morsels,
which the locals often enjoy just
as they come, washed down with
a cup of dark tea. *Ranginak* is a
glorious celebration of the fruit,
brought alive with the addition
of nuts and spices and offered
regularly at festive occasions as
a mark of hospitality.

STUART WEST (C) DORLING KINDERSLEY; TIM GERARD BARKER © GETTY IMAGES

RANGINAK

MAKES ABOUT 20 PIECES

Nutritious, delicious, addictive and just a little bit naughty, one piece of this moreish Iranian date cake, with its heady mix of nuts and spices, just won't be enough.

METHOD

1 Heat the walnuts in a pan over a low heat for about 2 minutes, until they become fragrant.

2 Stuff each date with pieces of walnut and set aside.

3 Place the butter in a pan over a low heat and allow it to melt completely.

4 While still over the heat, add the sugar to the melted butter and stir until it's dissolved, ensuring it doesn't burn.

5 Add the flour, keeping the mixture over a low heat, and stir regularly for about 15 minutes. It should be golden in colour and take on the consistency of a paste.

6 Remove from the heat.

7 Add the cardamom and cinnamon and mix again.

8 Spoon half of this mixture into the bottom of a serving dish and flatten across the base of the dish.

9 Arrange the stuffed dates in a single layer on top of the mixture.

10 Spread the remainder of the mixture over the top of the dates and smooth out with the back of a spoon so the dates are evenly covered.

11 Sprinkle the ground pistachios and the coconut (if you are using it) evenly over the top of the mixture.

12 Leave to cool before cutting into diamonds.

TASTING NOTES

From bustling bazaars to atmospheric teahouses, this toothsome date cake pops up everywhere in Iran. It may be served in slices, in diamonds or even as a roulade. However it comes, it packs a tasty punch. Plump dates are stuffed with toasted walnuts, which are then bathed in an unctuous, warm mixture of butter and flour infused with a sweet blend of cinnamon and cardamom. The kaleidoscopic combination of flavours is an evocative delight bringing the myriad colours and scents of the country to mind with every mouthful. Given the complexity of its flavour, *ranginak* is surprisingly simple to make. Create, then sit back and savour. For a full Iranian experience, enjoy with a cup of black tea on the side. ● *by Rebecca Law*

ORIGINS

Like the chilli, the potato was enthusiastically incorporated into the pantheon of Indian cooking ingredients after it arrived on Portuguese ships from the Americas. Pomegranates are a home-grown speciality, having sprouted since ancient times in the Hindu Kush. Drying pomegranate seeds for out-of-season use is also as old as the hills – most *anardana* is made from the *daru*, the tart wild pomegranate from which the sweet modern version was domesticated.

YOU'LL NEED

1 cup *anardana* (dried pomegranate seeds), soaked in water for 30 minutes

700g (25 oz) potatoes, peeled and cubed

2 tbs ghee (clarified butter)

2.5cm (1in) piece of **ginger root**, peeled and finely chopped

3 **garlic cloves**, peeled and finely chopped

1 yellow onion, peeled and finely chopped

1 tsp salt

1 tsp ground red chilli

¼ tsp ground **turmeric**

1 tsp ground coriander

½ tsp ground cumin

2 tsp jaggery (palm sugar)

fresh **pomegranate seeds**, to garnish

TRAVELLINGLIGHT © GETTY IMAGES

INDIA

ALOO ANARDANA

SERVES 4

Potato salad, Indian-style, *aloo anardana* comes
hot or cold but always delivers a tantalising jolt to the
taste buds with its mix of spices and dried pomegranate.

METHOD

1 In a pestle and mortar, grind the dried *anardana* seeds with the water used to soak them to make a coarse paste.

2 Boil the cubed potatoes until soft but still firm (about 15 minutes), then drain and set aside.

3 Heat the ghee in a pan and saute the ginger, garlic and onion for a few minutes.

4 Add the cubed potato, salt, chilli and spices to the pan and mix to coat the potatoes.

5 Cook for another few minutes, then add the *anardana* paste and jaggery and cook for 5 minutes more.

6 Serve garnished with fresh pomegranate seeds.

TASTING NOTES

Indian salads are a brave new world to the uninitiated; fresh vegetables are thin on the ground, replaced instead by unripe fruit, noodles, cooked potato and spices. In *aloo anardana*, potatoes are boiled in the same unceremonious way as for all-American potato salad, but then given a superfood power boost with dried pomegranate *arils* (the namesake *anardana*), soaked before use to wake the sleeping flavours. The cold version is dressed with a zesty mix of roasted spices and dried chilli; the hot version is well on the way to becoming *patatas bravas*, with the ingredients flash-fried together. With the modern love of all things fresh, it's not uncommon to see *aloo anardana* garnished with fresh pomegranate *arils*, for extra colour and tang. ● *by Joe Bindloss*

DANIELE ROMEO PHOTOGRAPHER © GETTY IMAGES

YOU'LL NEED

4 cups **Kakadu plums**
  (also available frozen and
  powdered)
sugar (quantity varies; see
  Method)
1 tsp finely grated **lemon** or
  orange zest
white vinegar, **salt** and
  chopped **chilli** to taste, if
  desired

ORIGINS

Known to Aboriginal people
as *gubinge*, Kakadu plums are
traditionally noted for their
medicinal properties as much as
for their taste. An easily available
bush food, the fruit is eaten raw
and the tree's inner bark used as
a poultice for wounds. More recently, the plums' extraordinarily
high level of Vitamin C has been
embraced by urban foodies
and the fruit incorporated into
gourmet bush-tucker menus.

DAVID HANCOCK © ALAMY

MAKES
4–5 CUPS

NORTHERN TERRITORY, AUSTRALIA

KAKADU PLUM SAUCE

Widespread through the woodlands of northern Australia, fresh-picked Kakadu plums make a refreshing snack out in the bush. Back home, preserve their delicious citrus tang in a sweet-and-sour sauce.

METHOD

1 Wash the fruit, then drain.

2 Place the fruit in a heavy pan and cover with water.

3 Stew on top of the stove until tender.

4 Place a colander over a bowl and pour the stewed fruit into the colander.

5 Push the stewed fruit through the colander with a metal spoon to remove the seeds.

6 Return the stewed fruit to pan.

7 Add 1 cup of sugar for each cup of stewed fruit.

8 Add the lemon or orange zest.

9 For a savoury sauce, add vinegar, salt and/or chilli to taste.

10 Bring to a rolling boil for 20 minutes or until the desired thickness is reached.

11 Spoon into clean, dry sterilised glass jars and seal.

TASTING NOTES

There's something special about eating wild-grown food for the first time. Imagine walking on a sunny morning at the start of the dry season in Australia's tropical north. A broad-leaved *Terminalia* tree offers welcome shade. On the ground underneath is a layer of small, olive-shaped, greenish-yellow, smooth-skinned fruit; choose those that are soft to touch. A large seed is surrounded by a thin layer of slightly fibrous flesh that zings in the mouth; it tastes like a shot of sun-filled energy. Collect a bagful, and back in the kitchen transform the fruit into sweet or savoury preserves that work as well with cold cuts as they do with desserts. Months later, enjoy memories of that morning walk, stored as a jar of bush goodness on the shelf. ● *by Virginia Jealous*

JONATHAN SHORT © STOCKFOOD

ORIGINS

Melburnians can hardly lay claim to being the first to mash avocado – surely that honour belongs to the Aztecs – but the city's chefs bring a fresh perspective on how to enjoy the humble fruit. The origins of smashed avocado is unclear; some sources state that Sydney chef Bill Granger created it, while Melbourne newspaper *The Age* credits local cafe Porgie + Mr Jones with being the first to offer the dish.

YOU'LL NEED

1 medium avocado, peeled and pitted
1 tbs extravirgin olive oil
squeeze of lemon juice, to taste
salt and ground black pepper, to taste
chilli flakes, to taste (optional)
4 slices thick sourdough, toasted
1–2 tbs white wine vinegar
4 eggs
80g (3oz) goat's cheese or fetta, roughly diced
1 bunch of watercress
1 tbs dukkah (Egyptian seed mix)
1 tbs fresh mint (or a herb of your choice), finely chopped
2 tbs tomato or beetroot relish, to serve

TASTING NOTES

Every weekend morning in Melbourne you'll find friends catching up over coffees and brunch, with patrons spilling out into cafe courtyards. The high standards Australians have come to expect are reflected in the quality of the food and coffee; dishes come beautifully presented, and chefs offer new takes on menu classics. While creativity is rewarded – expected, even – there are a few essential components of the classic smashed avo: crunchy sourdough; perfectly ripe avocado mixed with good-quality olive oil and seasoned well; salty cheese, preferably a local goat's cheese or Persian feta; watercress (for added superfood status); and some fragrant herbs, such as mint. The crowning glory is the perfectly poached eggs. ● *by Katie O'Connell*

SERVES 4

SMASHED AVOCADO WITH WATERCRESS

This quintessential Melbourne brunch element elevates avocado on toast to a whole new level, with the city's chefs combining simple superfood ingredients and fresh flavours to create a modern Australian classic.

METHOD

1 Roughly mash together the avocado, olive oil, lemon juice, salt and pepper and chilli flakes (if using) using a fork.

2 Divide the mixture into four portions and spread each thickly on a slice of toasted sourdough.

3 To poach the eggs, bring about 10cm (4in) of water to a simmer in a pan.

4 Add the white wine vinegar to the water and stir until a whirlpool forms.

5 Crack an egg into a cup or a ramekin.

6 Slide the egg into the centre of the whirlpool, folding the edges of the whites inwards to keep the egg together and to form a spherical shape.

7 Repeat with the remaining eggs, so they are all in the water.

8 Cook the eggs for 3–4 minutes, until the whites are set but the yolks are still runny.

9 Carefully lift out the eggs with a slotted spoon and place them on kitchen paper to dry.

10 Sprinkle the cheese over the avocado mixture on each slice of sourdough toast.

11 Cover with sprigs of watercress and sprinkle with dukkah and chopped fresh mint.

12 Top each portion with a poached egg.

13 Season with salt and pepper.

14 Serve with relish on the side, and enjoy immediately.

TIP *Use this recipe as a starting point; feel free to add your favourite extras, such as smoked salmon, or grilled tomatoes or mushrooms.*

PETER ADAMS © GETTY IMAGES

VEGETABLES

We're yet to meet a vegetable that is not good for us somehow. But, just like fruits (p76), some are mightier than others, and the manner in which veggies are prepared and eaten also plays a significant role in maximising their health benefits. A rise in vegetarian eating, as well as 'meat-free Mondays' for those unwilling to make the full commitment (we're not judging, meat has its merits, p138), demonstrates a trend towards the traditional days of 'meat and two veg' being over. Increasingly, vegetables are becoming the main players on the plate, with meat relegated to second banana. →

HISTORY

People have depended on vegetables since the times of Greek philosopher Socrates (and he was born in 469 BC). Plato's *Republic* extensively quotes Socrates and his insistence that the humble veg should form an essential part of our diet. However, specifics of when each vegetable came to be harvested for consumption varies. Cabbages originated in Europe before 1000 BC, beetroot from Germany or Italy in the Middle Ages, and aubergines from India before spreading to China then Europe in the 15th century. Little has changed looks-wise (though carrots were purple until the 17th century), except that we've wised up to their nutritional benefits.

HEALTH BENEFITS

A diet that includes a variety of multicoloured vegetables is your best defence against chronic disease, notably certain types of cancers. Vegetables contain vital nutrients for health and for the smooth functioning of your body. For minimal calories, you cannot get much more antioxidant bang for your buck than in the veggie patch. High veggie consumption reduces your risk of high blood pressure, heart disease, stroke, and can reduce the risk of kidney stones. Do not overcook vegetables, otherwise you leach away all the goodness and the colour. Steaming is the healthiest way to cook most types, or a quick little stir-fry in a wok.

SEAGULL, L. VISITBRITAIN/DANIEL BOSWORTH © GETTY IMAGES

DID YOU KNOW?

In Italy the aubergine (eggplant) is called *melanzane*, which means 'crazy apple'. This etymology dates back to ancient times when it was believed that anyone who ate too much eggplant would go mad. If you've tried *melanzane* in Italy you may see every deliciously crazy reason to overindulge. We say: everything in moderation.

VARIANTS

Just like fruits, vegetables are not sitting still when it comes to mixing things up in the expectations stakes. Some newer varieties that you might spot at your local farmers' market include the mouse melon (looks like a baby watermelon, is actually a cucumber/lime-flavoured, grape-sized vegetable). Or there's the downright exotic, such as the *oca*, native to the Andes of South America, also known as the 'New Zealand yam' (such is its popularity in that country): a colourful root veg that is an excellent source of Vitamin C, potassium and iron.

GREEN VEGETABLES

'Eat your greens!' Heard that before? Well, it's cited for good reason. Leafy greens, in particular, are riding Antioxidant Highway on a one-way ticket to Superfoodtown. It's very simple, it's all about the green colour. It means the vegetable is rich in chlorophyll, a pigment very similar to human blood. When a chlorophyll-rich food is eaten, the production of haemoglobin in the blood increases: this means more oxygen in the blood – exactly what cells need to survive. It's like a mini blood transfusion for your brain, immune system and your kidneys. In fact, there are way more superfood greens than we could cover here, but here are some superstars.

WATERCRESS

Our winner: the only vegetable given a perfect nutrient score of 100 by the US Center of Disease Control. Rich in 15 essential vitamins and minerals, watercress has more Vitamin C than oranges, more calcium than milk and more iron than spinach. It's close to being an anti-ageing miracle food.

CHINESE CABBAGE

Closely following watercress in the superfood ratings, stakes, Chinese cabbage is also known as Napa cabbage or Celery cabbage. It has highly anti-inflammatory properties, thanks to its cruciferous powers (see boxed text opposite page, top), as well as being high in calcium and iron.

CHARD

This veg comes in three varieties: green chard, Swiss chard and the delightfully vibrant rainbow chard. Super high in antioxidants, chard is rich in Vitamins A, C and K, as well as B-complex vitamins. Its high levels of nitrates have been shown to lower blood pressure.

FRANS ROMBOUT, CREATIV STUDIO HEINEMANN, WIN-INITIATIVE © GETTY IMAGES

CRUCIFEROUS VEG: THE CRUSADERS AGAINST DISEASE

A bowl of freshly steamed beet greens (the most nutritious part of a beetroot being the green leafy top that most people cut off and throw away!), drizzled with a little extra virgin olive oil, may not be everyone's idea of a superhero, but it's one of many cruciferous vegetables that can reduce your risk of heart attack, stroke and certain cancers. Your other cruciferous friends include cauliflower, cabbage, Brussels sprouts, bok choy, Chinese cabbage, collard greens, kale and watercress, among many others.

ASLI BARCIN; CREATIVEYE99; JOFF LEE © GETTY IMAGES

SPINACH
'Strong to the finish cause he eats his spinach', was the catch-cry of famous cartoon character Popeye the Sailorman, whose biceps would instantly bulge after he ate the green stuff. Respect, Popeye. Spinach is indeed a powerhouse of muscle-building iron.

COLLARD GREENS
A classic side dish from Southern USA (p124), collard greens are a cholesterol-lowering wonder when steamed. Like kale, they're full of nutrients that are great for bone health but contain more fibre, manganese, and twice as much iron and Vitamin B2.

KALE
Potentially overhyped but still loaded with more vitamins (K1, C and A), antioxidants and minerals (calcium and potassium) than most fruit and vegetables, kale is thought to aid cardiovascular health, protect eyesight and help prevent against some cancers.

OTHER SUPERVEG

BEETROOT

While their green tops are the best (see boxed text, p119), the actual beetroot is linked with the dilation of blood vessels and thus the lowering of blood pressure. It also contains compounds that help support detoxification of vital organs, such as the liver. The betalains (what gives these veg their purple colour) may help prevent cancer and other degenerative diseases.

AUBERGINE

Also known as the eggplant in North America and in Australia, these glamorous globes aren't always deep purple – they can range from black through to orange. Technically a fruit (but usually served as a veg), aubergines are lovely roasted or pureed into baba ganoush (an eastern Mediterranean dip). They're full of dietary fibre, potassium and B vitamins.

CAULIFLOWER

Often underestimated, yet increasingly turned into new and exciting dishes by the world's hottest chefs, the humble cauliflower contains many nutrients that may help prevent cancer, heart disease and stroke. It's also high in fibre, Vitamin C and folate. And don't just stick to white; keep an eye out for the purple, green and orange varieties.

BERGAMONT; SCIENCE PHOTO LIBRARY; BURKE/TRIOLO PRODUCTIONS © GETTY IMAGES

TAKE CARE COOKING CABBAGE

Aluminium utensils are no friend of the cabbage. The mustard oils in cabbage are great for warding off natural pests in the garden but they break down into sulphur compounds when cooked. This reaction intensifies with the metals in aluminium cookware, which can not only discolour your cabbage but make the flavour a bit intense and unpalatable, not to mention pretty smelly! Go for stainless-steel or enamelled cast-iron cookware instead.

CARROTS

Heard the rumours about carrots improving eyesight? It's all true. It's the beta-carotene that's converted to Vitamin A in the liver, which then combines with a protein called opsin to form rhodopsin. This is what you need for healthy night and colour vision. The Vitamin A and antioxidants in carrots can also protect skin from sun damage.

CREATIV STUDIO HEINEMANN © GETTY IMAGES, LOTTIE DAVIES © LONELY PLANET

ORIGINS

Turkish cooks have been stuffing leaves for longer than some civilisations have existed. The tradition of making *dolma* – literally 'stuffed things' – dates back at least as far as Ottoman times, and perhaps as far back as ancient Greece and Persia. One controversial theory credits the invention to the hill tribes of Azerbaijan, who were among the first nomads to settle down and raise their own vegetables.

MAKES ABOUT 20-30 SARMA

YOU'LL NEED

2 bunches of Swiss chard (20-30 leaves)
700g (25oz) minced lamb or beef
1 yellow onion, peeled and finely chopped
½ cup rice (uncooked)
2 tbs olive oil
½ tsp sugar
½ tsp ground black pepper
1 tsp cumin seeds
1 tsp chopped mint
1 tsp chopped parsley
1 tsp salt
plain Greek or Turkish yoghurt , to serve

TASTING NOTES

Stuffed vine leaves may be the vision of a Mediterranean mezze, but not everyone goes for the borderline fermented flavour and briny overtones. If you are making fresh-from-the-garden stuffed vegetables, why spoil all that goodness with something pickled in sea water? So swap preserved grape leaves for fresh-plucked Swiss chard, or *pazı*, trading heavy, salty flavours for a fresh dose of garden vitamins. *Sarma* come hot (with meat) or cold (often with raisins and pine nuts) but the key theme is simplicity – rice, onion, tomato, olive oil and a generous pinch of chopped parsley and mint. Turkish cooks can roll these little cylinders of perfection as tight as panatella cigars; home-made, they're lumpier but just as lovely. ● *By Joe Bindloss*

ANITA_BONITA © GETTY IMAGES

TURKEY

ETLI PAZI SARMA (DOLMA)

When it comes to healthy lunches, Turkish cooks are on a roll, literally, in the case of *etli pazı sarma* – delicate parcels of meat and rice rolled tightly in chard leaves.

METHOD

1 Trim the stems from the chard and wash the leaves.

2 Blanch the chard leaves for a few minutes in boiling water a few at a time, then remove them with a slotted spoon and immediately cool under running cold water in a colander. Set aside.

3 To create your *sarma* filling, combine the minced meat, chopped onion, rice, 1 tablespoon of oil, seasonings, spices and ½ teaspoon salt. Knead the mixture with your hands until thoroughly blended.

4 On a flat surface or chopping board, take one of your cooled, blanched chard leaves at a time, and trim away the thickest portion of the central stem.

5 Add a spoonful of the stuffing mixture to the middle of the leaf, fold both sides over the mixture, then roll from the bottom to create a tight cylinder, like a *dolma*.

6 As soon as each *sarma* is ready, place it in a shallow pan ready for cooking, with the overlapping edge facing down towards the bottom of the pan.

7 Arrange your *sarma* in neat rows until the bottom of the pan is covered (you can move on to a second layer if necessary), then add enough boiling water to cover the sarma by about 1cm (½in).

8 Drizzle over the remaining tablespoon of olive oil and sprinkle with the remaining ½ teaspoon of salt, then bring the water to the boil.

9 Cover and reduce the heat, then simmer very gently until most of the water disappears and the rolls are soft and tender.

10 Serve topped with plain Greek or Turkish yoghurt.

WHITWORTH IMAGES © GETTY IMAGES

SERVES 6

ORIGINS

This meal is a lasting legacy of the collision between Native American, African, and European culinary traditions in the Southern states. Greens were one of the crops that slaves were traditionally allowed to farm for themselves, and so it became a cornerstone of the Southern diet, along with the cheap, tasty and nutritious accompaniments of corn bread and black-eyed peas. These three dishes remain a staple in the South today.

YOU'LL NEED

For collard greens

3L (3 quarts) water
225g (½lb) ham hocks (about one small ham hock)
1 tbs coarse sea salt
1 tbs ground black pepper
1 tbs chipotle pepper sauce (Chipotle Tabasco pepper sauce for preference, or a smoked hot pepper sauce)
1 large bunch collard greens, washed (if unavailable, try kale or mustard greens, but reduce the cooking time)
2 tbs apple cider vinegar pepper sauce to serve

For black-eyed peas

450g (1lb) dried black-eyed peas, washed and soaked overnight, then rised well
3 cups water
450g (1lb) smoked ham hocks
1 tsp salt
½ tsp ground black pepper

For buttermilk corn bread

2 tbs bacon drippings or butter
1½ cups corn meal
½ cup plain (all-purpose) flour
1½ tsp bicarb soda (baking soda)
1 tsp salt
2 eggs
1¼ cups buttermilk, plus more if needed

TASTING NOTES

Collard greens are a hallmark of Southern cooking, and you can find as many interpretations of this dish as there are restaurants and home cooks. Greens should be tender and served with enough of its own cooking juice, known as 'pot liquor', to allow you to sop up its slightly bitter jus with a chunk of hot, buttered corn bread. Pepper sauce (a seasoning made of hot peppers pickled in vinegar) is the customary accompaniment, as it cuts the sharp flavour of the greens with its vinegary heat and acidity. Enjoy this dish sitting on a porch with a Mason jar full of iced tea to experience the way this meal has been served for the last two centuries. ● By Rebecca Warren

BRENT HOFACKER © ALAMY

THE SOUTH, USA

COLLARD GREENS WITH BLACK-EYED PEAS

Collard greens have a piquant flavor that pairs perfectly with the buttery tang of crumbly corn bread and the creamy, savoury taste of black-eyed peas.

METHOD

For collard greens

1 In a large pan, bring the water to the boil and add the ham hocks, salt and pepper, and chipotle pepper sauce. Reduce the heat to medium and cook for 1 hour.

2 Strip the leaves from the tough stems of the greens. Stack about six of the stripped leaves together, roll them up and cut them into thin strips. Repeat until all leaves are cut into strips.

3 Place the greens in the same pan with the ham hocks and add the apple cider vinegar.

4 Cook for 45–60 minutes, stirring occasionally, until the greens are tender.

5 Serve warm, topped with pepper sauce.

For black-eyed peas

1 Place the soaked (and thoroughly rinsed) peas in heavy pan and cover with the water. It should come 5cm (2in) above the peas.

3 Add the ham hocks. Bring to a slow boil and then reduce to a simmer.

4 Cook for about 2 hours until peas are tender. Top up with water as needed.

5 Remove the ham hocks from the pan. Take the meat from the bones and shred with a fork. Return to the pan, and season to taste.

6 Serve warm. Top with a dollop of mayonnaise, if desired.

For buttermilk corn bread

1 Preheat the oven to 190°C (375°F). Put the bacon drippings in a 25cm (10in) cast-iron skillet and place the pan in the oven.

2 Combine the dry ingredients in a bowl.

3 Mix the eggs and milk, then stir into the dry ingredients. If the mixture seems dry, add another 1–2 tablespoons of buttermilk.

4 When the fat and the oven are hot, remove the skillet from oven, pour the batter into it and smooth out the top. The batter should sizzle when it hits the skillet.

5 Return the skillet to the oven. Bake for about 30 minutes, until the top is lightly browned and the sides have pulled away from the skillet; a toothpick inserted into the centre will come out clean when it's done. Serve hot.

YOU'LL NEED

3 cups spinach leaves (*palak*)
2 cups boiling water, salted
2.5cm (1in) piece of ginger root, finely chopped
2 green chillies, deseeded
½ cup water
2 tbs ghee (clarified butter)
1 cup (8oz) paneer, cut into 2.5cm (1in) pieces
1 tsp cumin seeds
1 onion, peeled and finely chopped
4 garlic cloves, peeled and chopped
1 tomato, finely chopped
¼ tsp turmeric powder
salt, to taste
½ tsp garam masala
3 tbs double cream
1 tsp fenugreek leaves
nann or rice, to serve

ORIGINS

Palak paneer made it on to menus via the *dhabas* of the Punjab, the family-run roadhouses that have catered to generations of truck drivers hauling loads along the Grand Trunk Road. However, the true origins of the dish go back at least as far as the Mongols, who discovered the technology behind cheese-making while charging across the Hindu Kush with leather saddle-bags full of souring milk.

SOHADISZNO © GETTY IMAGES; MATT MUNRO © LONELY PLANET

INDIA

PALAK PANEER

SERVES 4

Break up the oily *dopiazas* and *bhunas* with saintly *palak paneer* – India's palate-cleansing curry of spinach, ginger, turmeric and curd-cheese.

METHOD

1 Wash the spinach leaves and drain.

2 Finely chop the spinach, then blanch in lightly salted water for a few minutes.

3 Drain the spinach and transfer to cold water, then drain again.

4 Blend the drained spinach in a food processor with the ginger, chillies and ¼ cup of water.

5 Heat 1 tablespoon of the ghee in a pan, and lightly fry the paneer cubes until they start to brown.

6 Remove the paneer from the pan and set aside to drain on a piece of kitchen towel.

7 Add the remaining ghee to the pan, then fry the cumin seeds until aromatic (2 minutes).

8 Add the chopped onion and garlic, then saute lightly for about 10 minutes, until the onion is soft

9 Add the tomato and fry until soft.

10 Next, add the turmeric, the spinach puree and a generous pinch of salt.

11 Add remaining water and simmer for 5 minutes, adding extra salt to taste if needed.

12 Add the garam masala and paneer and simmer for a few more minutes.

13 Finally, stir in the cream and add the fenugreek leaves.

14 Serve with naan or rice.

TASTING NOTES

What strikes the taste buds most about this inspired combination of spinach and mustard leaves, curd cheese and spices is the comparative simplicity of its flavours. Where other curries are a circus of tastes, *palak paneer* offers subtlety and a hint of yogic calm. The pureed spinach leaves provide healing notes of chlorophyll and iron – and a break from the usual monotone colour palette of browns and umbers – and the hunks of paneer serve as miniature palate cleansers between each mouthful. Of course, this is still India, so the sauce has all the expected zing – the earthiness of turmeric, the fresh medicinal tang of ginger, scene-setting *jeera* (cumin) and the exotic tones of garam masala. ● *By Joe Bindloss*

BON APPETIT © ALAMY

ORIGINS

This traditional English dish grew out of necessity: finding a use for leftover vegetables from a roast dinner. The earliest recipe dates back to the early 19th century – its name relating to the sound of the cabbage cooking. The dish's popularity grew during the period around World War II when food rationing was mandatory. Meat from the roast was often included, but it's left out more often these days.

SERVES 4

YOU'LL NEED

butter, for greasing
150g (5oz) Brussels sprouts
150g (5oz) dark green cabbage, shredded
2 tbs olive oil
200g (7oz) carrots, peeled and chopped
200g (7oz) parsnip, peeled and chopped
250g (9oz) squash, peeled, deseeded and chopped
400g (14oz) potatoes, peeled and chopped
½ tsp paprika
pinch of ground black pepper
1 tbs white wine vinegar
pinch of salt
4 very fresh medium eggs
75g (3oz) watercress

TASTING NOTES

It's early afternoon on Boxing Day and a general feeling of slothfulness pervades the house, though it's matched in equal parts with growing pangs of hunger. The latter wins over and two lightbulbs spark when the fridge door opens, one in the fridge itself, the other in your head as you realise you have the makings of a rather tasty (and healthy) meal. Cabbage, carrots, and mashed potatoes are usually key players, and Brussel sprouts are often a favourite too. The collision of these earthy flavours is a sweet one, even better if some squash is involved. And when it's browned with olive oil, seasoned with paprika and a little pepper, and topped with a poached egg and some watercress, you have a happy home. ● *By Matt Phillips*

BUBBLE AND SQUEAK WITH POACHED EGGS AND WATERCRESS

This veggie superfood-laden dish traditionally flashes on the radar come Christmas, when the fridge overfloweth with leftovers, but it's great for a comforting meal year-round.

METHOD

1 Preheat the oven to 220°C (425°F).

2 Grease a small (25 x 35cm; 10 x 14in) roasting dish.

3 Steam the Brussels sprouts until they are bright green and tender, about 6–8 minutes.

4 Steam the shredded cabbage for about 5–8 minutes.

5 Steam the root vegetables until soft, but not mushy. Drain and leave to steam dry.

6 Pound the cooked root vegetables and Brussels sprouts in a large bowl using a potato masher.

7 Add the cabbage and the olive oil, then season with a sprinkling of paprika and black pepper.

8 Spread the mixture in the greased roasting dish and bake on the oven's top shelf for 20–30 minutes (it's done when crispy on top).

9 Bring a small pan of water to the boil then reduce it to a simmer, and add the vinegar and a pinch of salt.

10 Crack the eggs individually into a ramekin or cup. Stir the simmering water to create a gentle whirlpool, then slowly tip each egg into the vortex, white first. Leave to cook for 3 minutes.

11 Remove the eggs with a slotted spoon, and cut off any wispy edges using the edge of the spoon. Drain on kitchen paper.

12 Cut the baked root vegetable and cabbage into sections, and top each serving with a poached egg and sprigs of watercress.

TIP *You can also make bubble and squeak traditionally by frying roasted leftover veg, but we've used a healthier alternative: steaming unroasted vegtables before baking the mixture.*

YOU'LL NEED

4 cups water
4 fresh beets, scrubbed
2 large potatoes, peeled and
  cubed
½ head of white cabbage,
  chopped thinly
1 yellow onion, peeled and
  chopped
2 carrots, peeled and grated
4 tbs cider vinegar
4 tbs lemon juice
1 tbs brown sugar
¼ tsp salt
6 cups beef stock
3 tbs sunflower oil
2 dried bay leaves
¼ tsp ground black pepper
1 tbs dill, chopped
sour cream or *smetana*,
  to serve

ORIGINS

The great-great-grandfather
of modern borsht was a dish of
humbling simplicity – just a crude
broth made from the pickled
stems, leaves and flowering
umbels of marsh hogweed. The
Ukrainians and Poles probably
have the strongest claims
to being the true fathers of
borscht; the first record of the
dish in Russia came in a 16th-
century homemaking treatise,
which exhorted Russians to turn
their gardens over to hogweed
and share the soup made from it
with the poor.

BILL BACHMANN © ALAMY, ANETA_GU © GETTY IMAGES

RUSSIA AND UKRAINE

BORSCHT

SERVES 4

Russia's most famous dish is so much more than cabbage soup; it's a fermented flavour infusion, packed with more vitamins than an athlete's kitbag.

METHOD

1 Fill a large soup pan with the water and boil the beets until soft (this may take up to an hour).

2 Remove the beets and allow to cool.

3 Once the beets are cool, peel and slice into thin strips.

4 Use the leftover beet water to boil the potatoes for 15 minutes or so, until soft.

5 After the potatoes have been cooking for 10 minutes, add the cabbage.

6 In a separate pan, fry the onion and grated carrot in oil until soft.

7 Stir in the vinegar, lemon juice, sugar and salt to the carrot and onion mixture.

8 Add the beef stock and bay leaves to the pot with the cabbage and potato.

9 Add the carrot and onion mix and stir until combined.

10 Add the ground black pepper and chopped dill.

11 Simmer on a medium heat until all the vegetables are cooked.

12 Serve topped with a spoonful of sour cream or *smetana*.

TASTING NOTES

These days, you'll be hard pressed to find borscht made with the traditional hogweed, though it is experiencing a minor resurgence on modern Russian restaurant menus. Instead, the 21st-century version is prepared with fermented beetroot, which gives the dish both its pungent aroma and its vivid, blood-on-the-snow hue. The other ingredients added to this full-flavoured, almost alcoholic base are textures as much as flavours: cabbage, carrot, potato, onions, parsley root, tomatoes, even apples and beans in some more adventurous recipes. And all this with a nutritious beef-bone stock to pack in essential vitamins. The taste of borscht is unmistakably central European: almost beer-like, slightly sour, faintly alkaline, and so obviously packed with nutrients that you can almost feel the goodness flowing into your immune system. ● *By Joe Bindloss*

YOU'LL NEED

½ cup bulgur wheat
1 cup boiling water
200g (7oz) ripe tomatoes, diced
2 spring onions (scallions), finely sliced
½ cup (4oz) flat leaf parsley, roughly chopped
½ cup (4oz) fresh mint leaves, roughly chopped
juice from 1 lemon
3 tbs olive oil
salt, to taste
1 head of romaine lettuce

ORIGINS

For many, tabbouleh is the first introduction to the flavours of the Levant, usually as part of an Arabic mezze. In fact, the dish goes back to the earliest days of wandering Middle Eastern nomads, who foraged for the ingredients to make *qadbat* – a prototype salad of wild Levantine herbs. The Lebanese spread the dish as far as Cyprus and even, surprisingly, Dominican Republic, while the Ottomans ensured its permeation across the entire Middle East.

BRETT STEVENS; TIME E WHITE © GETTY IMAGES

SERVES 4

LEBANON

TABBOULEH

Nothing says Middle East quite like the fresh, herbal tones of tabbouleh, the mint and parsley salad that adds magic to every mezze.

METHOD

1 Wash the bulgur wheat in a sieve until the water comes clear, then drain.

2 Add the bulgur wheat to a bowl and pour over the boiling water, then cover with cling film and leave to soak for at least half an hour.

3 Dice the tomato and finely slice the spring onion and set aside.

4 Combine the mint and parsley leaves with the tomato and spring onion.

5 Drain the bulgur wheat for a second time, then add to the mixture of herbs and vegetables.

6 Pour on the lemon juice and olive oil and season with salt to taste.

7 Mix thoroughly with your hands and serve with fresh romaine lettuce leaves.

TASTING NOTES

In the feeding frenzy of an Arabic mezze, tabbouleh could easily get lost in the flurry of flavours, but this is a dish worth sampling without distractions. Try it at lunch, sitting in the shade of a gnarled pistachio tree, feeling the warm earth under your toes below the table. Eschew corner-cutting variations using couscous for the Levantine original, made using *salamouni* bulgur wheat grown on the slopes of Mount Lebanon. The grains form a superstructure on which the flavours of the salad can build; powerful herbal tones of parsley and mint, the salty freshness of tomato, astringent onion, and of course, the tang of lemon and olive oil. Eat it scooped up on small romaine lettuce leaves, which provide a crisp, clean counterpoint to the mingling flavours. ● *By Joe Bindloss*

YOU'LL NEED

2 garlic cloves, peeled and
  crushed
150mL (⅔ cup) olive oil
3 slices of day-old white
  sourdough bread, cut into
  crouton-sized cubes
2 anchovy fillets
1 egg yolk
juice of ½ lemon
2 heads of romaine lettuce,
  torn into rough pieces
handful of finely grated
  Parmesan

ORIGINS

Caesar Cardini, the Italian
immigrant credited with
this salad's invention, was
flummoxed on a busy American
Independence Day in 1924
when his kitchen in Tijuana
ran short of ingredients. He
pooled together what he had,
and the original Caesar salad
was born. Anchovies have since
replaced Worcestershire sauce
in most recipes, and the salad
is no longer finger food – it was
designed to be eaten that way,
one leaf at a time.

JEREMY WOODHOUSE/HOLLY WILMETH; RICK POON © GETTY IMAGES

SERVES 4

CAESAR SALAD

Salty and tangy, crispy and crunchy, this salad assaults the palate on several fronts – all of them positive. Egg, anchovies and the mighty romaine lettuce provide superfood power.

METHOD

1 Let the garlic infuse in the olive oil for at least an hour.

2 Preheat the oven to 200°C (400°F).

3 Toss the sourdough cubes in a bowl with a little of the oil.

4 Bake for approximately 15 minutes on a tray in the oven until crisp and golden brown.

5 In the salad bowl, mash the anchovies with a fork into a paste.

6 Beat in the egg yolk, before gradually pouring in more of the garlic-infused oil, until it reaches your desired thickness.

7 Finish the dressing by stirring in the lemon juice.

8 Add the romaine to the salad bowl.

9 Toss well, add the Parmesan and then toss again.

10 Top with the croutons and serve.

TASTING NOTES

The salty, tangy and savoury nature of the anchovies permeates the salad, much more so than the original recipe's simple use of Worcestershire sauce. The sharpness of the lemon, and the richness from the Parmesan add a depth to the flavour, while the crunch of the garlic-infused sourdough croutons makes the perfect accompaniment to the moist, crisp romaine. From its humble, if accidental, beginnings in Tijuana, this salad has spread around the globe, and is now found everywhere from New York to London and Sydney. Grilled chicken is often offered as an optional topping, as are capers and bacon. ● *By Matt Phillips*

ORIGINS

I love that in the Middle East they put so many herbs and spices in their food, so I wanted to recreate the same sort of flavours with this salad. I was also really inspired by Persian chef and author Sabrina Ghayour – she encouraged me to use various spices in my cooking, and this led to me including cinnamon and cumin in the yoghurt dressing, which simply transformed the dish. It's my Middle Eastern take on the traditional potato salad.

ENGLAND

MIDDLE EASTERN POTATO SALAD

With its spicy soul in the Middle East, and its heart in rooted in the West, this simple sweet potato and pomegranate salad really punches with worldly favour.

YOU'LL NEED

For salad
2 large (550g) sweet
  potatoes, unpeeled
Drizzle of sunflower oil
pinch of salt
10g parsley, chopped
pomegranate seeds, to
  garnish

For dressing
½ tsp ground cinnamon
1 tsp ground cumin
¼ tsp Himalayan pink salt
250g goat's or sheep's milk
  yoghurt

METHOD

1 Preheat the oven to 180°C (350°F)

2 Quarter the unpeeled sweet potatoes lengthways.

3 Put the sweet potatoes on baking tray and drizzle with sunflower oil, adding a pinch of salt. Roast for 25-40 minutes, until soft. Remove from the oven and leave to cool.

4 Make the dressing by mixing the cinnamon, cumin, salt and yoghurt together.

5 Arrange the cooled sweet potato on a platter, pour the dressing over it and sprinkle with the chopped parsley.

6 Serve with a salad or as a side dish, garnished with the pomegranate seeds.

TASTING NOTES

Served cold, the roasted sweet potatoes have the most wonderful caramelised sweetness, which is balanced by the sour notes of the chopped parsley and yoghurt dressing. These flavours are then complemented by the dish's Middle Eastern influences: cumin and cinnamon. The textures are just as diverse, from the softness of the sweet potato to the hard pomegranate seeds, which pop in your mouth. The wonderful aromas of the spices send you on an instant journey to faraway lands. ● *By Natasha Corrett. Recipe from* Honestly Healthy in a Hurry.

© LISA LINDER

UNCLEDMITRO © GETTY IMAGES

FISH & MEAT

Hello, devotees of the Paleo diet, we know we're preaching to the converted in this section. Others may be surprised to see 'meat' listed with long-touted superfood fish. But yes, meat can be a superfood; organs, in particular, are the most nutritious part of an animal, as proponents of nose-to-tail eating will attest. The secret with both meat and fish is to focus on quality and sustainably raised produce. Eating fish and lean meat several times a week is highly recommended for a multitude of health reasons, just watch portion sizes with meat: favour a fist-sized serving rather than a plate-sized steak for a healthier heart. →

HISTORY

Humankind has been eating meat for millions of years. Our earliest ancestors hunted game for survival under relatively precarious conditions. But, as animals bred, human lifestyles became more sedentary, as meat became easier to access. The eating of fish dates back around 40,000 years to the Paleolithic period (no prizes for guessing where the Paleo diet got its name...). Analysis of human remains from this time confirms the regular consumption of freshwater fish. The ancient Egyptians also fished the River Nile, drawings and paintings depicting the activity as quite the hobby.

HEALTH BENEFITS

There's one uniting factor across the broad spectrum of meat and fish, and that's protein. The complete proteins in these foods supply all the amino acids our bodies need to generate our own protein. Apart from soybeans (p17), no other food source comes close to replicating this nutritional aspect of meat and fish. The benefits of eating oily fish are well documented; quite often our diets are lacking in the nutrients they provide. If you've ever heard fish referred to as 'brain food', it's because fish are the best source of Omega 3 fatty acids, and one of these fish Omega 3s is responsible for strengthening brain cells and protecting them from disease. Be mindful, though, that many fish contain high levels of mercury, which can be toxic if overconsumed (see boxed text, p143 for more).

JUSTIN FOULKES © LONELY PLANET

MATT MUNRO © LONELY PLANET

DID YOU KNOW?

In Japan, the *fugu* or puffer fish is a high-risk delicacy. It contains a deadly poison called tetrodotoxin, but is reportedly so delicious it's worth the culinary gamble with mortality. Non-toxic preparation of the puffer fish is governed by strict Japanese law; don't dream of trying this dish unless you see a special *fugu* chef licence mounted on the restaurant wall.

VARIANTS

The different ways fish are caught have an effect on both their taste and how healthy they are for you. The same deal goes for meat: what animals are fed and how they are raised creates noticeable differences in the colour, texture, level of fat, and the taste of what ends up on your plate. In the same way that deep-fried fish and chips, while a charming seaside treat occasionally, is not a superfood meal, processed meat is also a no-no on a regular basis. In fact, bacon lovers received some bad news in late 2015, with the World Health Organization concluding that consumption of processed meats increases the risk of colorectal cancer. On the upside, they agreed that eating meat (fresh, not processed) 'has known health benefits'. So read on!

FISH

Not all fish are created equal. While we're constantly being told to eat more fresh fish (two servings a week, ideally), only some fish are stratospheric in the superfood arena. When researchers noticed that the Inuit, who eat mostly oily fish, had fewer heart attacks and strokes than the average person, investigations into purported health benefits truly began. Ready for this? Oily fish (such as salmon, mackerel and sardines) may help prevent heart disease, rheumatoid arthritis, strokes, prostate cancer, age-related vision loss, dementia, blood clotting, and the anti-inflammatories they contain help with skin conditions (such as eczema and psoriasis). Investigations into the evidence are ongoing.

SALMON

Rich in Omega 3 fatty acids, salmon also contains essential minerals, such as iron, phosphorous and calcium, along with vitamins A, B and D. It's also one of the best sources of selenium, which, in small doses, stimulates healthy hair and nail growth. Go for wild-caught or canned salmon over those that are farmed in pens. Pacific chinook and sockeye are fattier than pink and chum varieties.

SARDINE

These tiny fish punch above their weight in nutritional value. They are one of the most concentrated sources of Omega 3s, and are excellent for bone health (more calcium than cow's milk). Consumption also helps regulate mood and brain function, thanks to their iron, zinc, magnesium, selenium, B and D vitamins. Fresh or tinned (watch the salt) on sourdough toast, they make a great way to start the day.

TUNA

Even canned tuna delivers richly with the Omega 3s, but choose your species of tuna and monitor your intake carefully (see boxed text, opposite page, top). Recent research has revealed that a compound of selenium in tuna called selenoneine defends tuna against free radicals, with researchers believing it performs the same function in humans as an antioxidant, helping prevent chronic diseases.

PACI77; GEOFF KIDD; ALLE12 © GETTY IMAGES

EATING FISH WITH ENVIRONMENTAL AWARENESS

One-third of the world's fisheries are close to collapsing, so it's important to choose wisely and sustainably when purchasing fish. It needs to be both good for you (that means without toxins) and the environment. For example, bluefin tuna is on the World Wildlife Fund's endangered species, list and, due to high mercury levels, the European Food & Safety Authority recommends limiting tuna intake in general. The US-based NRDC also recommends avoiding top predator species such as king mackerel, marlin, swordfish, shark and both bigeye tuna and yellowfin tuna (also known as 'ahi'), again because of their elevated mercury levels.

MACKEREL

One of the prettiest fish, this glowing blue-striped beauty is not just rich in Omega 3s and protein, but also coenzyme Q10, which is a powerful antioxidant thought to provide a lot of energy in the body. Look for Atlantic chub mackerel when shopping – king mackerel should be avoided due to its potentially high mercury levels, and pregnant or nursing mothers should restrict the amount of Spanish mackerel in their diet.

MUSSEL

The superfood of shellfish, mussels are very high in protein and low in fat. In fact, the green-lipped mussel from New Zealand is thought to be more beneficial to joint mobility than fish oil supplements. The blue or common mussel is the one you'll usually find in other parts of the world, however, but it's also high in Omega 3 fatty acids. Underutilised, mussels rank highly with regard to sustainability.

ANCHOVY

The size of this wee fish is inversely proportional to the strength of its flavour, hence why it lands atop pasta dishes and pizza, and within salad dressings (p134). Loaded with Omega 3 fatty acids, anchovies are also categorised by the NRDC as a species with the least amount of mercury contamination. High in magnesium, phosphorus and calcium, the anchovy is also great for maintaining strong bones.

SCIENCE PHOTO LIBRARY; FLOORTJE; FRANS ROMBOUT © GETTY IMAGES

MEAT

We're not giving you a free-for-all pass on all meat here. Oh no. Go for lean, grass-fed meat over grain-fed meat where possible. Given there is almost eight times more saturated fat in conventionally fed beef, grass-fed meat is so nutritious it's almost a different food. Grass-fed beef or chicken has more of the good fats (namely, Omega 3 and Omega 6) than corn-fed. Omega 3s, in particular, improve your mood, concentration and fire up your metabolism. In addition grass-fed beef's linoleic acid is thought to reduce stomach fat while increasing muscle. That's a meat marvel.

LIVER

The most nutritious organ, liver contains iron and Vitamin B12 as well as many other B vitamins, Vitamin A and folate. Liver is renowned for its mysterious anti-fatigue qualities, something scientists have yet to rationalise. If you find offal confronting, try and ease your way in with a smear of liver pâté on a nice wedge of crusty bread.

LEAN RED MEAT

With highly absorbable nutrients, lean cuts provide an abundance of Vitamin B12, iron, zinc and Vitamin D. Kangaroo is one of the best supermeats, given it is always free-range, has higher protein and zinc levels than other red meat and double the iron of fish. Meat from grass-fed animals has up to four times more Omega 3s.

CHICKEN

Organic, free-range chicken is a naturally lean meat (the breast is the leanest) and it contains less saturated fat than most red meat. While chicken itself is not widely renowned as a superfood, there truth behind the tales about the antioxidant and anti-inflammatory powers of chicken soup (p96), which is thought to boost immunity.

TATIANA VOLGUTOVA, ALEXEYBORODIN © GETTY IMAGES

TOM PARKER BOWLES: WHY MEAT IS A SUPERFOOD

Renowned food writer, restaurant critic and *Esquire* food editor Tom Parker Bowles recently penned a carnivorous call-to-arms called *Let's Eat Meat*. Rather than advocating a flesh-eating orgy, he sensibly argues for an eat-less-but-higher-quality approach. We asked him why he champions meat as a superfood.

'Packed with protein, stuffed with flavour and, if you're lucky, run through with lovely fat, meat is the ultimate superfood. It has built civilisations, constructed empires and provided carnivorous succour to billions. Who can argue with the restorative powers of a charred steak, the life-affirming properties of a roast, or the sheer delectably visceral joy of stew, daubes, pies, braises and bakes. Forget coconut and kale. For true superfood, go with the magic of meat.'

LEAN TURKEY

While the butter-slathered roast bird at Thanksgiving or Christmas with the high-fat stuffing may be the centrepiece of celebrations, it's less healthy for your heart. But a lean piece of skinless turkey breast is not just high in protein but also tryptophan, which is converted into serotonin, known as the body's mood-boosting hormone.

GBH007: MASKOT © GETTY IMAGES

ORIGINS

Archaeological digs tell us that humans have consumed mussels for thousands of years, and given the fact that this delectable treat grows in abundance (and is considered to be underutilised), it may be around to feed us for millennia more. It's no surprise that the grape-loving French were the ones to transform the mussel into a delicacy with wine, and it was such a hit that *Moules marinières'* popularity quickly outgrew France's borders.

YOU'LL NEED

2kg (4.5lb) fresh mussels
100g (3.5oz) unsalted butter, cubed
4 French shallots, peeled and diced
300mL (10 fl oz) dry white wine
4 sprigs of thyme, leaves picked
2 bay leaves
bunch of flat leaf parsley, chopped finely
salt and ground black pepper, to taste
French baguette, to serve

TASTING NOTES

There's a bit of a chill on, with the wind blowing off the English Channel. Stepping into an atmospheric eatery with a roaring fire may start to thaw your extremities, but the best cure to warm your insides is a steaming bowl of *moules marinières*. The gorgeous freshness of the mussels in combination with the subtle sweetness of the shallots and the acidic dry white wine is soothing on so many levels. Many recipes also call for cream, which mellows the flavours but adds richness to the sauce. There's no need for utensils, simply use one of the empty shells as a pincer to pluck the lovely morsels from the other mussels. Mopping up the sauce with a fresh French baguette is only icing on the proverbial cake. ● *by Matt Phillips*

DAWIDKASZA © GETTY IMAGES

NORMANDY, FRANCE

MOULES MARINIÈRES

Superfood meets fast food. Yes, really. This classic dish from Normandy may take humble mussels to a higher level, but it won't take you long to get them there.

SERVES 4

METHOD

1 Rinse the mussels in running cold water before scraping off any barnacles or dirt. Don't scrub them as this may cause the shells' colour to leach out during cooking, turning the juice an unappetising shade of grey. You'll need to throw away any with broken shells. If any are open, give them a sharp tap: if they remain open, you'll need to bin them too.

2 Remove the little fibrous beards (the appendages that the mussels use to attach themselves to the rocks) by pulling them sharply towards the mussel's hinge. Let the mussels sit in cold water for a couple hours

3 Melt the butter in a large saucepan. Add the diced shallots and cook for 8–10 minutes until translucent in colour.

4 Add the wine and bring to a simmer. Reduce the heat and cook gently for a further 5 minutes.

5 Drain the mussels.

6 Turn up the heat to medium-high, then add the mussels as well as the thyme and bay leaves. Cover and cook for around 3 minutes (until most mussels have opened).

7 Add the parsley and give the pan a good shake to mix.

8 Remove any mussels that are still closed.

9 Season lightly and serve straightaway in a bowl, together with the liquid.

TIP *The freshness of the mussels is paramount. A fresh mussel is tightly closed, heavy with seawater and shiny. There should be no fishy smell.*

JUSTIN FOULKES © LONELY PLANET

MATT MUNRO © LONELY PLANET; RUA CASTILHO © STOCKFOOD

ORIGINS

The Inca marinated fish to cook them, but used *chicha*, a fermented corn drink, rather than the citrus that features these days. Spanish conquistadors brought the limes that became bona fide ceviche marinade. Corvina, prevalent on Peru's coast, became traditionally used. Japanese-Peruvian chef Dario Matsufuji shook up a century-old recipe and reduced marinating time from hours to minutes in the 1970s, which became the preparation method to emulate.

YOU'LL NEED

1 red onion, peeled and thinly
 sliced
500–675g (1–1½lb) sea bass
 fillets, skinned and chopped
 into large, bitesized pieces
pinch of red chilli flakes
1 garlic clove, peeled and
 grated
juice of 5 limes
500g (1lb) sweet potatoes,
 peeled and diced
1 corn on the cob, chopped
 into 5cm (2in) pieces
5 tbs olive oil
3 tsp rice vinegar
¼ tsp caster sugar
½ *ají limo* (use normal red
 chilli pepper if unavailable),
 deseeded and chopped
grated rind of 1 lime
2 small avocados, peeled,
 stoned and sliced
3 tbs chopped coriander
 leaves (cilantro)
salt and ground black pepper,
 to taste

SERVES 6 AS A STARTER

PACIFIC COAST, PERU

CEVICHE DE CORVINA

Combining the marinated fish and chilli peppers the Inca would have known, zesty Spanish-introduced citrus and a makeover from a Peruvian-Japanese chef, Peru's national dish is the ultimate fusion cuisine.

METHOD

1 Lay half the red onion in a large glass bowl with the fish on top. Sprinkle over the chilli flakes and grated garlic. Cover with lime juice.

2 Cover the bowl and chill. Professional ceviche-makers in Peru now use the quick marinade which, when preparing large quantities, helps keep the fish fresh, but this is an acquired art and a 2-hour marinade is recommended for home cooks. During the chilling/marinating process, spoon the lime juice over the fish again once or twice.

3 Boil the sweet potatoes for 10 minutes, then add the corn. Cook together for 5 minutes. Drain and place to one side.

4 Whisk together the oil, rice vinegar and caster sugar until smooth. Then whisk in the chopped *ají limo*/chilli pepper and grated lime rind.

5 When the fish is done, drain and discard the lime juice.

6 Add the fish to the oil/rice vinegar/caster sugar and mix well. Add the diced sweet potato and avocado and mix again.

7 Add the remaining red onion along with the coriander leaves and the corn on the cob pieces and season to taste. Serve immediately.

TASTING NOTES

The sharp kick of the lime, the crunch of red onions and the fiery red-yellow of Peruvian chilli pepper *ají limo* mingle with the taste of soft white corvina (a Pacific sea bass) as it breaks into chunks in your mouth. Then your palate grasps the sweet potato and corn that counterbalance the feisty fish with an earthiness that reminds you what a unique thing *ceviche de corvina* is in a country where most street snacks are carbohydrate-dominated. Unlike many street foods, presentation is also key. The onion-and-chilli-pepper garnish sits on top of the fish, encircled by the sweet potato, corn clumps and hunks of avocado. Proper ceviche is an assault on the eyes as well as the taste buds. ● *by Luke Waterson*

YOU'LL NEED

340g (12oz) salted herring fillets

½ cup Swedish spirit vinegar or white wine vinegar

1 cup water

⅔ cup fine white sugar

12 whole peppercorns

10 juniper berries, sliced

10 whole cloves

1 bay leaf

1 small red onion, peeled and diced

2 small horseradishes, peeled and diced

2 medium carrots, peeled and thinly sliced

¼ cup dill, roughly chopped, to garnish

ORIGINS

Herring is ubiquitous in Northern Europe but with the Baltic Sea teeming with them, Swedes have pickled this fish since medieval times. On Sweden's west coast, just north of Gothenburg, the tiny island of Klädesholmen is the country's 'herring capital'. This centuries-old fishing community's heyday was during *den stora sillperioden* (the 'great herring period'), around 1748–1808. Today, it's home to pickled herring company Klädesholmen Sill and a herring museum.

MATT MUNRO © LONELY PLANET

SWEDEN

PICKLED HERRING

Simultaneously salty, sweet and spicy, *inlagd sill* (pickled herring) is a dish that encapsulates Sweden's pristine coastal waters and seafaring traditions, and is a mainstay of any Swedish *smörgåsbord* (buffet).

METHOD

1 Cover the salted herring fillets in cold water and leave overnight, changing the water once (late at night or early in the morning).

2 Put the vinegar and water in a pan with the sugar.

3 Heat over a medium heat until the sugar has dissolved.

4 Add the peppercorns, juniper berries, cloves, bay leaf, onion, horseradish and carrot and remove from the heat.

5 Leave the pickling mixture to cool, then transfer it to a non-reactive (non-metal) bowl.

6 Drain the herring fillets and add them to the pickling mixture.

7 Cover the bowl with cling film and refrigerate for 72 hours, stirring occasionally.

8 Remove the herring from the pickling mixture and pat dry with kitchen paper.

9 Cut the herring into 1.25cm (½in) slices.

10 Place the herring on a serving platter and ladle over some of the pickling mixture.

11 Garnish with dill and serve.

TIP *Variations on pickling styles include a smothering of mustard marinade. Just don't mistake pickled herring for surströmming (fermented Baltic herring), which is soaked in brine and continues fermenting after it's been canned – its overpowering smell has caused buildings to be evacuated (seriously).*

TASTING NOTES

Pickled herring's intricate sweet and sour flavours and silky and supple textures mean that this Swedish staple works with simple accompaniments such as boiled potatoes, hard-boiled eggs, cheese such as a Cheddar-style *Prästost* or sharper, crumblier *Västerbottensost*, and sour cream. The luxurious oiliness of the fish is a perfect match for dark rye crisp bread – another dish invented as a means of preservation. Herring is an exceptionally healthy fish, containing essential fatty acids, antioxidants, vitamins and minerals, as well as being low in saturated fat and calories (and it is environmentally sustainable too). ● *by Catherine Le Nevez*

MELANIEMAYA © GETTY IMAGES

ORIGINS

In a country of 1200 desert islands, fish is bound to be the key feature on the menus. People are also bound to find inventive ways of serving it. The traditional basis of *mas huni* was the enigmatically named 'Maldive fish' – hunks of tuna, boiled, smoked and dried to the texture and colour of aged driftwood. Once cured, Maldive fish lasts almost indefinitely, making it the perfect food for long sea voyages.

YOU'LL NEED

For the mas huni

4 fresh green chillies, finely chopped
2 large white onion, peeled and finely chopped
juice and zest of 4 limes
salt, to taste
600g (22oz) Maldive fish or canned tuna in brine, drained
2 cups grated fresh coconut
extra lime wedges and a handful of coriander leaves, to garnish

For the roshi

3 cups plain (all-purpose) flour
salt, to taste
4 tbs vegetable oil
1 cup boiling water

TIP Mas huni *is easy to make, but Maldive fish is hard to get hold of outside the Maldives and Sri Lanka; canned tuna is a good substitute.*

TASTING NOTES

The setting is everything when sampling *mas huni*. Eschew the five-star hotel breakfast buffets for the modest setting of a ramshackle Maldivian teahouse in Male, the Maldives' miniature capital. Here you'll find all of the varied and wonderful morsels that are collectively known as *hedhika*, or 'short eats'. Alongside assorted sauces and fritters, you are guaranteed to find *mas huni*, served with a pile of freshly roasted *roshi* and a cup of sweet tea – the perfect pick-me-up after a hard night of hauling fishing nets and landing your catch on the beach at sunrise (it's also good after a morning of sunbathing). As for the flavour, it's exactly what you would expect – salty, tangy, fishy, spicy – the kind of dish that Robinson Crusoe would have invented, only to discover that Man Friday's people had been making it for centuries. ● *by Joe Bindloss*

MALDIVES

MAS HUNI

SERVES 4

**A spicy Maldivian seafood salad with all the goodness
of the Indian Ocean distilled into a brunch – perfect when
you've just come back from a day of strenuous island-hopping.**

METHOD

1 To prepare the *mas huni*, crush the chillies, onion, lime juice and zest, and salt together in a mixing bowl.

2 Flake in the Maldive fish or drained tuna.

3 Stir in the grated coconut – use fresh meat, not desiccated coconut.

4 Leave the mixture to steep for a few minutes.

5 Meanwhile, make the *roshi*. Sift the flour and salt into a bowl.

6 Add the oil, then pour on the boiling water little by little, stirring as you go, to form a soft dough.

7 Leave the dough until it is cool enough to touch, then turn it out on to a lightly floured surface.

8 Knead the mixture for 10–15 minutes, until it is soft and elastic.

9 Divide the dough into six balls.

10 Roll each ball flat with a rolling pin.

11 Heat a heavy frying pan over a medium heat.

12 Cook a dough circle in the dry frying pan, flipping it once the *roshi* starts to rise up and cooking it on the other side until it is ightly browned.

13 Remove the dough circle to a plate once it is cooked and cover it with a dish towel to keep it warm while you repeat the cooking process with all the dough.

14 To serve the *mas huni*, pack some into a small bowl.

15 Invert the bowl on to a serving plate to form a mound of *mas huni* in the centre.

16 Repeat with the remaining mixture.

17 Serve the *mas huni* with a wedge of lime and a few coriander leaves to garnish.

18 Eat the *mas huni* under a palm tree (if you have one close by), with the warm *roshi*.

ORIGINS

Danish influence popularised
open sandwiches in Greenland,
but local flavours reign supreme.
In remote Greenland, food
follows the cycle of the seasons.
Summers are spent in a frenzy
of food preparation: endless
daylight facilitates long hunting
expeditions, fishing trips and
foraging sprees for herbs and
berries. This dish contains all the
elements required to protect
the body against the brutal
Greenlandic winter.

BENJAMIN HAAS © GETTY IMAGES, BJARKI REYR MR © ALAMY

SERVES 2-4

GREENLAND

GREENLANDIC OPEN SANDWICH

In this Greenlandic twist on Denmark's *smørrebrød* (open sandwich), fragrant angelica and smoky halibut combine elements of the land and sea, typifying the clean flavours of this remote island.

YOU'LL NEED

1 tsp angelica leaves
pinch of salt
1 cup butter, softened to
   room temperature
4 large slices dark rye bread
150g (5½oz) smoked halibut
   (or trout, salmon or cod)

METHOD

1 Finely chop the angelica leaves.

2 Blend the chopped angelica, salt and butter in a small bowl with a wooden spoon until it is smooth.

3 Spread about 1 teaspoon of the angelica butter on to each slice of the rye bread. (Store the remaining butter in your fridge, or wrap small portions and freeze them for later use with baked meat or fish.)

4 Top each slice of buttered rye bread with a generous helping of smoked fish.

TASTING NOTES

Angelica grown in Greenland's harsh climate develops a distinct flavour – sweet, musky, with a whisper of anise. The scent is so strongly evocative of Greenland that expats say it rouses pangs of nostalgia for home. The first bite of this dish is infused with angelica, which lends fragrance to the salty chewiness of the halibut. The nutty flavour of rye bread gives an earthy note to each mouthful. The size of your serving will depend on the time of year, as extremes of light and dark force Greenlanders to follow seasonal rhythms. In summer's glare, when the sun barely dips below the horizon, Greenlanders eat light meals, work long hours and hike the wilderness (for fun or food). In winter, hearty meals sustain families through the permanent darkness. ● *by Anita Isalska*

ORIGINS

Popular across Scotland, this traditional soup has its roots in the fishing village of Cullen on the Moray Firth. 'Skink' is an old word for 'shin of beef', which became synonymous with a cheap soup. However, in this part of Scotland – where fish was more plentiful – cooks decided to replace the meat with fish and thus this much-loved classic came into being.

YOU'LL NEED

knob of butter
1 medium onion, peeled and finely chopped
2 medium potatoes, skins on, cut into chunks
1 bay leaf
120mL (4fl oz) good chicken stock
500g (1lb 1 oz) undyed smoked haddock
1 leek, cut into chunks
568mL (1 pint) full-fat milk
120mL (4fl oz) single cream
salt and ground black pepper, to taste
parsley, chopped, to garnish
crusty bread and butter, to serve

CRAIG EASTON © LONELY PLANET. SIMON REDDY © ALAMY

SERVES 4

SCOTLAND

CULLEN SKINK

**One of the world's finest seafood soups, Cullen skink
pulls the flavours of the earth and sea together in
a hearty haddock chowder that packs a real punch.**

METHOD

1 Melt the butter in a large pan over a medium heat.

2 Add the chopped onion and cook for about 10 minutes, until transparent but not browned.

3 Add the potatoes, bay leaf and chicken stock to the pan and simmer for 10–15 minutes, until the potato is cooked.

4 Remove the bay leaf and lightly mash the potatoes against the side of the pan using a fork.

5 In a separate pan, poach the haddock and leek in the milk over a medium heat for about 5 minutes, until the fish is opaque and cooked and the leeks are just tender.

6 Remove the fish from the milk and gently flake it, removing any bones.

7 Add the milk, leeks and fish to the potato mixture, stir well to combine and cook for a further 5 minutes.

8 Add the cream and season to taste with salt and pepper.

9 Sprinkle with chopped parsley and serve with crusty bread and butter.

TASTING NOTES

Smooth and comforting and infused with a deep smokiness, Cullen skink is one of those dishes that are easy to make but hard to perfect. Very fresh fish is essential, as are floury potatoes and the best stock. The finished result should have a rich taste of the sea layered with the sweetness of slow-cooked onions and the silkiness of starchy potatoes and cream. A wholesome yet indulgent dish, the smoothness can be counterbalanced by leaving some chunks of fish or potato intact if you prefer a meatier texture. Cullen skink is best enjoyed by the seaside, ideally with a view over a harbour where brightly coloured fishing boats bob in the water against a backdrop of stone harbour walls, brooding clouds and craggy islands on the distant horizon. ● *by Etain O'Carroll*

UNCLEDMTRO © GETTY IMAGES

ORIGINS

Literally translated, *gravlax* means 'buried or grave salmon', a name that refers back to the Middle Ages when fishermen would salt freshly caught salmon and then bury it in the sand above the high-tide line to preserve it for the freezing winter ahead. Today, the briny flavour is achieved by burying a fillet of raw salmon in a dry marinade of salt, sugar and dill and letting osmosis work the flavours into the fish.

YOU'LL NEED

For the gravlax

2 x 500g (17oz) sushi-grade salmon fillets, skin on
1 tbs black or white peppercorns
2 tbs caster sugar
4 tbs sea salt
½ cup dill
rye bread, to serve

For the dill and mustard sauce

2 tbs Dijon mustard
2 tbs soft light brown sugar
2 tbs cider vinegar
pinch of salt
2 tbs vegetable oil
4 tbs dill fronds, finely chopped

TASTING NOTES

No Nordic celebration would be complete without a lavish fish-based buffet and no *koldtbord* (Norway's equivalent of the Swedish *smörgåsbord* would be complete without an offering of gravlax. It comes second in the proceedings, being eaten after the opening herring dishes. The melt-in-your-mouth salmon against the dense and nutty rye make a perfect partnership of textures while the aniseedy fronds of dill add freshness and sparkle. It is a pivotal part of Christmas and Easter feasts, when friends and family gather together around a large table strewn with delicacies of the sea, drink shots of *snaps* between courses and make merry singing traditional *snapsvisor* (drinking songs). ● *by Helen Brown*

NORWAY

GRAVLAX ON RYE BREAD WITH DILL AND MUSTARD SAUCE

SERVES 8

This Nordic specialty consisting of slices of cured salmon served with dill and mustard sauce on a bed of rye showcases the bounty of Norway's crystal-clear fjords with mouth-watering effect.

METHOD

1 Put one of the salmon fillets skin side down in a large rectangular dish.

2 Crush the peppercorns in a pestle and mortar, then mix the crushed peppercorns, sugar and salt together.

3 Lay half of the dill on top of the salmon in the dish. Spread the salt, sugar and peppercorn mixture over the top of the salmon and dill. Add the remaining dill on top.

4 Lay the second salmon fillet (skin side up) on top of the one already marinating.

5 Cover the salmon with a board and weigh it down with something heavy so all the ingredients are tightly bound.

6 Refrigerate for 2 days, turning the fish every 12 hours to be sure the brine entirely bastes the fish.

7 After 2 days, remove the salmon (now gravlax) from the brine, scraping off any excess with a blunt knife.

8 Cut the gravlax on the bias into medium-thin slices (these are traditionally thicker than slices of smoked salmon), leaving the skin behind.

9 To make the sauce, put the mustard, brown sugar, cider vinegar, salt, vegetable oil and dill in a blender or food processer and blend until smooth.

10 Serve a few slices of salmon on top of each piece of rye bread in open sandwiches. Dress with the dill and mustard sauce or allow your guests to add their own.

NIGEL PAVITT © GETTY IMAGES

TUNED_IN © GETTY IMAGES

ORIGINS

The word *skrei* originates from the Norse word *skrida*, meaning to wander – and this is a journey that begins in the Barents Sea.

Between January and April huge numbers of *skrei* migrate back to their northern Norway spawning grounds, and Norwegians have been intervening this pilgrimage for centuries, snapping up a select percentage. *Skreimølje* exemplifies the fishing community's time-tested waste-not, want-not mentality, utilising the *skrei* in its entirety.

YOU'LL NEED

For skrei *liver*

300g (10oz) liver of skrei (cod), chopped into small pieces
1 tsp salt
1 tsp vinegar
ground black pepper, to taste
1 tsp freshly squeezed lemon juice
2 cups water

For skrei *roe*

500g (1.1lb) roe of skrei (cod)
2 cups water
½ tsp salt

For skrei

4 cups water
salt, to taste
1.5kg (3lb) fresh skrei (cod), filleted and sliced

For accompaniment

5–6 small potatoes per person
1 egg per person
fresh parsley, chopped

TASTING NOTES

Norway's strict catching and selection criteria ensure only the very best *skrei* reach consumers' palates. The ostensible difference with the *skrei* in *skreimølje* over a cod supper in any other nook of the world is in the sharp, pure white of the fish flesh. But this is off-set by the equally distinct faded grey-pink hue of the roe. In the mouth it's more about feel than taste – the *skrei's* juicy softness, the roe's grainy rubbery consistency. The acidity of the liver lingers a while, but the waxiness of the potatoes and egg soothes all. Best consumed on a dark mid-winter day in a Norwegian fishing port... ● *by Luke Waterson*

NORWAY

SKREIMØLJE

Skrei is an exceptionally succulent, seasonal Arctic Norwegian cod: when sliced, salted and boiled then served with its liver, roe and sides of boiled potatoes and eggs it is transformed into *skreimølje.*

METHOD

1 Begin by preparing the *skrei* liver (as this takes longest); clean the liver thoroughly of membranes and, once chopped, place in a saucepan.

2 Add the salt, vinegar, ground black pepper and lemon juice and mix well.

3 Add the water and bring to the boil.

4 Remove the pan from the heat and allow the liver to soak for 20 minutes.

5 Next, prepare the *skrei* roe; clean and wrap it in greaseproof paper to prevent separation during boiling.

6 Place the wrapped roe in the water with salt and bring to the boil, then turn the heat down to the lowest setting and allow to simmer for 20 minutes.

7 Boil the small potatoes and eggs in two separate pans.

8 Now, prepare the *skrei* itself. Boil the water, seasoned well with salt (a guideline would be a ½ cup salt per litre of water, but season according to taste).

9 Once the water has boiled, remove the water from the heat and add the slices of filleted *skrei*, then bring to the boil again.

10 Set the pan aside and let the fish stand for 5 minutes. Remove the slices from the water, cover and keep warm until the liver, roe and potatoes/eggs are ready.

11 Serve the *skrei*, liver and roe on a plate. Arrange the boiled potatoes, garnished with chopped parsley around the *skrei*.

12 Peel the hard-boiled eggs and slice, then arrange them on the plate.

MATT MUNRO © LONELY PLANET

SARAH BOSSERT © GETTY IMAGES

ORIGINS

Seafood has probably always been eaten raw in Polynesia, particularly by fisherman who often spent several days at sea and had no choice in the matter. The Japanese introduced the idea of *sashimi* (eaten in French Polynesia as a heap of thinly sliced raw tuna on a bed of rice) in the last century while European and Chinese cultures brought their own vegetables and spices to the islands during early contact.

TASTING NOTES

Sweet from the coconut, tart from the lemon, savoury from the fish, *poisson cru* is as refreshing as a tickle of trade wind. It's usually prepared by Polynesian hands and ladled into plastic takeaway dishes alongside a heaping portion of steamed rice. It's eaten for dinner at a *roulotte* (mobile food van), among families sharing the dish alongside *steak frites* (steak and chips) and chow mein, the night sticky with smoke from open-air grills. The rice soaks up the coconut flavour of the sauce and softens the crunch of the vegetables; the raw tuna takes on the texture of a firm *mousse torte*, tender and silky. The scent of flowers adds the final touch to gustatory paradise. ● *by Celeste Brash*

SERVES 4–6

FRENCH POLYNESIA

POISSON CRU

If flower-scented air and turquoise lagoons could be blended into a dish, *poisson cru* would be it: raw fish and vegetable salad dressed with lime juice and coconut milk.

YOU'LL NEED

500g (about 1lb) fresh yellowfin tuna, cut into 2.5cm (1in) cubes (salmon, bonito and other deep-water fish can be used)
¾ cup fresh lime or lemon juice (or a mixture of both – they shouldn't be too sour)
2 tomatoes, chopped
½ small onion, peeled and finely chopped
1 cucumber, finely chopped
1 carrot, grated
1 green pepper, deseeded and thinly sliced
1 cup coconut milk
salt and pepper, to taste
scallion or parsley, chopped

METHOD

1 Soak the tuna chunks in a bowl of seawater or lightly salted fresh water (locals swear this makes the fish more tender) while preparing the vegetables.

2 Remove the tuna from the salt water and place in a large salad bowl. Add the lemon or lime juice and leave the fish to marinate for about 3 minutes.

3 Pour off about half to two-thirds of the juice (depending on how tart you like it), then add the vegetables and toss together with the fish.

4 Pour the coconut milk over the salad and add salt and pepper to taste.

5 Garnish with chopped spring onion or parsley and serve with white rice.

MATT MUNRO © LONELY PLANET

ORIGINS

Pho has its origins in the cuisines of France and China and was popularised around the end of the 19th century. The Vietnamese took the rice noodles from their northern neighbour and a taste for red meat from the colonialists, and created something new. Some say *pho* (pronounced 'feu') is derived from the French dish *pot au feu*, while others argue that it is Chinese in origin, stemming from a Cantonese word for noodles, *fan*.

YOU'LL NEED

For the broth

10cm (4in) piece of ginger root
2 yellow onions
cooking oil
2.25kg (5lb) beef marrow or oxtail bones
4.75l (5 quarts) water
1 cinnamon stick
1 tsp coriander seeds
1 tbs fennel seeds
5 star anise
2 cardamom pods
6 whole garlic cloves
¼ cup fish sauce
2 tbs sugar
1 tbs salt

For the noodles & garnishes

225g (½lb) beef steak
450g (1lb) dried flat rice noodles
10 sprigs mint
10 sprigs coriander leaves (cilantro)
10 sprigs Thai basil
12 sawtooth coriander leaves
½ yellow onion, peeled and thinly sliced
2 limes, each cut into 6 wedges
2–3 chilli peppers, sliced
450g (1lb) beanshoots
hoisin and hot chilli sauce

TASTING NOTES

Dawn is breaking across Vietnam and the hum of scooter engines has yet to reach its mid-morning crescendo. The *pho* sellers have set up stalls, some little more than a battered collection of metal pans, while others include plastic tables and gleaming trolleys. Whatever you choose, it's the broth that matters. This is the heart and soul of *pho* and should be rich and deeply flavoured, hinting at star anise, cardamom and coriander. The noodles should be freshly made, while the chillies are mild, rather than fierce. Beanshoots add a satisfyingly crunchy texture. A dash of fish sauce, a squeeze of lime, and breakfast is ready. Grab a wobbly chair, sit back and slurp. ● *by Tom Parker Bowles*

SERVES 8

PHO

The breakfast of champions, this fragrant spiced Vietnamese noodle soup topped with slices of beef, brisket, chicken or meatballs and a squeeze of lime is the perfect wake-up call.

METHOD

For the broth

1 Halve the ginger and onions lengthwise and place on a baking sheet. Brush with cooking oil and put on the highest rack under a heated grill (broiler). Grill on high until they begin to char. Turn over to char the other side for a total of 10–15 minutes.

2 Boil enough water in a large pot to cover the beef bones and continue to boil on high for five minutes. Drain, rinse the bones and rinse out the pot. Refill the pot with the bones and the 4.75L of cool water. Bring to the boil, then reduce to a simmer. Remove any scum that rises to the top.

3 Place the cinnamon stick, coriander seeds, fennel seeds, star anise, cardamom pods and garlic cloves in a mesh bag (alternatively, *pho* spice packets are available at speciality Asian food markets) and add to the broth pot along with the charred onion and ginger and the fish sauce, sugar and salt and simmer for 1½ hours.

4 Discard the spice pack and the onion and continue to simmer for another 1½ hours.

5 Strain the broth and return it to the pot. Adjust the salt, fish sauce and sugar to taste.

For the noodles & garnishes

1 Slice the beef as thinly as possible across the grain.

2 Cook your noodles according to the packet.

3 Bring the broth back to the boil.

4 Arrange all the other garnishes next to your serving bowls.

5 To serve, fill each bowl with noodles and raw meat slices. Ladle the boiling broth into the bowls – this will cook the beef slices.

6 Garnish with the remaining herbs, onion, lime wedges, chillies, beanshoots and sauces, and serve immediately.

YOU'LL NEED

For the stew
500g (1.1lb) of frozen roasted
  reindeer
2 tbs lard
100g (3.5oz) butter
150mL (5 fl oz) beer (or water)
1 cup fresh (wild) mushrooms
  or ¾ cup dried mushrooms
salt, to taste

For the mashed potatoes
1kg (35oz) floury potatoes
100g (3.5oz) butter
100mL (3 fl oz) whole milk
salt and pepper, to taste

For the crushed lingonberries
2–3 tbs lingonberries per
  person
1 tbs honey

ORIGINS

Finnish cuisine has always been
about forward planning: snow
smothers the ground two-thirds
of the year, so it was a matter of
gleaning what you could, when
you could, and conserving it for
the tough times ahead. Conse-
quently a palette of distinctive
tastes was fostered, such as
roasted reindeer sliced thin
while still frozen and cooked in
butter before being garnished
with crushed lingonberries
and sugar.

SOILUUSSILA © GETTY IMAGES, GARY LATHAM © LONELY PLANET

FINLAND

REINDEER STEW WITH LINGONBERRIES

Take arguably the world's most nutritious red meat, prepare it *käristys* style (sliced part-frozen and simmered in butter) and, served as stew with Lapland mashed potatoes and lingonberries, you have Finland's quintessential hearty hunger-buster.

METHOD

1 Partially defrost the roasted reindeer at least 4–6 hours prior to preparing. Once partially defrosted, cut into thin slices and set to one side.

2 Heat the lard in large saucepan over a medium heat.

3 Add the sliced reindeer meat and fry until golden-brown.

4 Add the butter and mix well.

5 Add the beer (use water instead if desired).

6 Add the mushrooms. If using the dried mushrooms, allow these to soak for 15 minutes in water prior to adding.

7 Mix well, lower the heat, cover and simmer for 3 hours.

8 While the meat is cooking, defrost the lingonberries if using frozen lingonberries (if using fresh lingonberries, discount this instruction).

9 Peel and dice the potatoes and cook in salted water until soft, then drain and mash with the butter, milk, and salt and pepper to taste.

10 Crush the lingonberries with a spoon to release the flavours and add honey to taste.

11 Serve the stew and the mashed potato on separate parts of the same plate. The lingonberries can be served separately and then added according to individual taste.

TASTING NOTES

To maximise the chances of perfectly prepared reindeer, gravitate north: Lapland's capital Rovaniemi rustles up memorable versions of the dish. The freshly frozen meat should be dark, almost inky in colour with a taste best described to the first-timer as somewhere between liver and beef. Reindeer should never be drowned amid other strong flavours when cooked: butter and salt are all you need. This is therefore a somewhat minimalist stew; mushrooms are added as much for texture as taste and serving it with mashed potato is a textural decision too: stodge to mop up rich reindeer tastes. Crimson-coloured lingonberries, tart members of the cranberry family, lend that stab of sweet, saved-up summertime freshness. ● *by Luke Waterson*

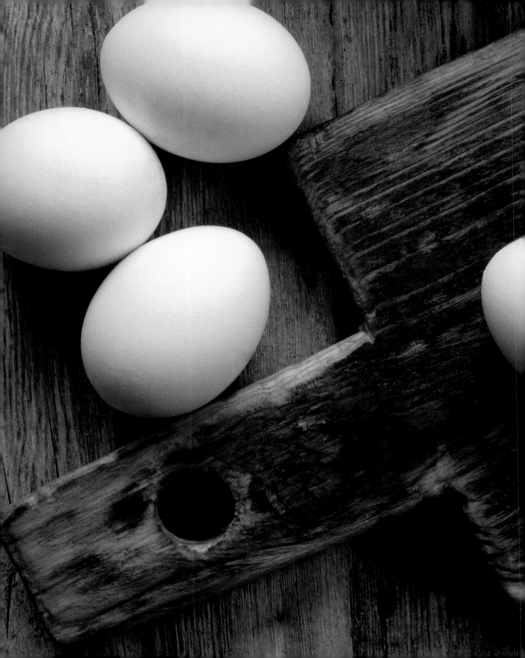

VITAKOT © GETTY IMAGES

OTHER SUPERFRIENDS

Far from being unmentionables or indefinables, these are the superfoods that didn't fall neatly into the previous categories, but are too important to ignore. You'll find a mixed bag of goodness in this section, some ingredients a little wackier than others (bet you didn't see plankton coming) while others are a cause for celebration. →

MATCHA

Green tea has been praised for its antioxidant levels for over a decade now, but matcha is on another level altogether, with one glass providing 10 times the amount of nutrition found in a cup of green tea. And unlike regular green tea, which is processed and the leaves left to dry in the sun, matcha leaves are never heated and are kept in the shade, preserving the natural nutrients. It also comes in a vibrant green powder, which is stirred into warm liquids rather than boiled or left to brew, like tea leaves or teabags. Part of Japanese culture since the 12th century, one teaspoon of matcha contains six times the antioxidants of goji berries (p80) and 60 times the antioxidants found in spinach (p119).

LOTTIE DAVIES © LONELY PLANET, DIANA TALJUN © GETTY IMAGES

KEFIR

This fermented yoghurt milk drink is a relatively new superfood, despite being a common healthy beverage in post-Soviet countries. Originating from the Caucasus region at the border of Europe and Asia, kefir (from the Turkish word 'keif', which means 'good feeling') has a slightly bitter taste but is winning fans for its probiotic qualities. It has loads of healthy bacteria and yeasts that are nourishing for the digestive system, which helps minimise bloating. Buy it by the bottle at major health food stores (it comes in various flavours, such as coconut, mango and vanilla) or make kefir cheese yourself (p178). While it is a dairy product, it actually helps improve lactose digestion, as well as healing inflammatory bowel disease, improving immunity and building bone density.

COCONUT OIL

It's no accident that *Simply Nigella*, Nigella Lawson's cookbook, is awash with cold-pressed coconut oil. It's currently considered the best cooking oil to use at high heats, despite its high saturated fat levels (which means it's yet to get a tick of approval for your heart health). Still, its high lauric acid levels supposedly counteract this, thought to boost good cholesterol levels in the body and to help fight infection. While studies are underway into claims it can boost memory power and potentially help patients with Alzheimer's and Parkinson's disease, it's certainly a superfood to watch.

DIMITRIS STEPHANIDES; MAGONE © GETTY IMAGES

BEE POLLEN

If pollen is used by bees as energy (in addition to honey), then why shouldn't humans harness this high-protein power too? And bee pollen's healing properties impressed Hippocrates 2500 years ago, long before the word 'superfood' was ever invented. Bee pollen has been considered a nutritious tonic in Chinese medicine for some time and it is actually richer in protein than any animal source.

MATT MUNRO © LONELY PLANET, MARC O. FINLEY © GETTY IMAGES

EDIBLE INSECT OIL: THE NEW WAVE OF COOKING OILS?

Pass the cooking-oil aisle of your supermarket and you'll be overwhelmed with choice. Along with heart-healthy olive oil (best used in salad dressings or sauteing vegetables over a medium heat, due to its lower smoking point), there's avocado oil, hemp seed oil, rice bran oil, red palm oil, chilli oil. But are you ready for cricket oil? Or grasshopper oil? That's right, researchers in the Netherlands are currently analysing oils from insects, as they are believed to be rich in fatty acids and a good source of protein.

EGGS

Eggs have been the unfortunate victim of two distinct phases: the 'eat no more than one egg a week because the cholesterol will give you a heart attack' falsehood and the fastidious 'egg-white-only omelette' craze. The entire egg is good for you, as often as you like. Egg protein helps build muscle strength because of its high levels of the amino acid leucine. Always buy free-range, and organic where possible.

DARK CHOCOLATE

Chocolate is a superfood! But only the dark kind, and by that we mean at least 70 per cent cacao (p16). Dark chocolate increases your serotonin and endorphins (a real mood booster, but you probably knew that). It's also rich in fibre, Vitamin B, iron, manganese, copper and magnesium, the latter being excellent for concentration. One study showed it had more antioxidant activity than açaí berries (p81).

SEAWEED

Already loved by many (usually wrapped around sushi), seaweed is a concentrated source of calcium and iodine. The latter is particularly important, given that the majority of women are deficient in iodine, which the body needs to make thyroid hormones: vital for healthy metabolism function and regulating body temperature. Buy organic where possible as seaweed absorbs pollutants in water in which it grows.

STOCK,KLAR, ROSEMARY CALVERT, SUPERIMMORY © GETTY IMAGES

THE RAW FOOD MOVEMENT

You may have heard of the rise in 'raw food' diets. The notion of eating food in its most natural state is gathering popularity, though be aware of the pros and cons to this approach. The nutritional benefits of eating unprocessed, locally sourced, living foods cannot be argued with. Yet eating predominantly (or only) raw food can be more irritating to some digestive systems. In addition, some vegetables, such as tomatoes (p80) are also much healthier for you when cooked.

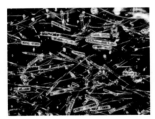

SPIRULINA

Often used in juice bars in 'green' smoothies, spirulina is a blue-green algae that has been a protein source for centuries, notably for ancient Aztec and African communities. Spirulina has loads of iron, as well as Vitamins B1 and B2, which is a sure-fire recipe for energy. As-yet-unproven studies suggest that it may also stop the growth of oral cancer cells.

PLANKTON

Plankton or 'marine phytoplankton' may sound like something you'd feed your pet fish. And while it's not particularly pleasant-tasting, just like spirulina, it's a nutritionally potent algae, and one that's only recently making waves in health-food stores. It's bought in a powder and is excellent for restoration of the liver, cell regeneration, boosting energy, and brain and heart health.

KIMCHI

Like kefir (p170), *kimchi* is another fermented superfood. It's a spicy Korean mixture of vegetables that have been fermented with healthy bacteria. It usually consists of cabbage, red peppers, onions, garlic and salt. You'll find it in the fridge of health food shops, as it needs to be kept cold to preserve its natural probiotics. It's a rich source of Vitamin C and very detoxifying for the liver.

BAIBAZ; SCENICS AND SCIENCE; 4KODIAK © GETTY IMAGES

LEMON MYRTLE

The lemon myrtle is an Australian tree with powerful antioxidant qualities. Sold as tea, powder, essential oil, and spices (the leaves contain more health benefits than the fruit or flowers), it's used in a variety of ways: for antiseptic qualities, treating colds, sore throats, upset stomachs and viruses. It's also high in calcium, zinc, magnesium and Vitamins A and E. Oh, and it's refreshingly lemony, of course.

DAVE KING © GETTY IMAGES, IAN HALLMAN © LONELY PLANET

ORIGINS

Matcha is the tea you'll
experience at a Japanese tea
ceremony, though it hails from
Tang-dynasty China. The ritual
elements grew out of Buddhist
monk preparations of the tea
and were imported to Japan
around the 12th century. For the
rest of the millennium, Japan
developed a strong love for and
cultural bond with the powdered
tea, though in recent years it has
returned to China and travelled
to other parts of the world as a
sought-after superfood.

SERVES 1

JAPAN

MATCHA GREEN TEA

It's the ultimate tea, unique at almost every stage of its life. Grown in shade, the leaves are deveined, destemmed, steamed, dried and then ground to a fine pure leaf powder – not your average cuppa!

YOU'LL NEED

2 tsp of **matcha green tea** powder
½ cup hot water, boiled but left to cool for a few minutes

METHOD

1 Place a small mesh strainer/sifter over a bowl and spoon the matcha powder into it.

2 Force the tea through the strainer with the back of a teaspoon – you want the dusty powder to fall through to the bottom of your bowl.

3 Add the hot water to the bowl and with a small whisk, blend the powder with the water till you have a light bubbly froth on your tea.

TASTING NOTES

The Zen calm of a Japanese tea ceremony adds a distinct flavour to the drinking experience, but when it boils down to it, it's the tea you're tasting. It's a confounding and intoxicating aroma that starts the process, slightly musty yet fresh and bright. The almost milky lime-green tea hits you first with a little bitterness, then you move through the vegetal layers of flavour you'd expect from a plant-based concoction. You might be reminded of the ocean, perhaps seaweed. That complex blend of bright fragrance and earthy must fades to a light sweetness and before you know it, you've brought the cup to your lips for more. It's addictive stuff. ● by Ben Handicott

WESTEND61; TDUBPHOTO; ANTHONY MURPHY © GETTY IMAGES

YOU'LL NEED

2 tbs **kefir grains**

4 cups milk (can be one of cow, goat, sheep or coconut)

ORIGINS

Kefir seeds, or 'grains of the Prophet', are said to have been a gift from Mohammed to the people of the Caucasus, with instructions to guard the grains closely. By the 19th century, Russian scientists, intrigued by the rumoured health benefits of kefir, were determined to discover more. In 1908, in an act of culinary espionage, Irina Sakharova finally acquired some seeds for Moscow; it's thought that all true kefir seeds in the world today have come from these.

MAKES
2 CUPS

NORTH CAUCASUS

KEFIR CHEESE

Made from fermented milk, the flavour of slightly sour, creamy-textured kefir cheese evokes its origin in herders' huts of ancient central Asia. More recently – and more conveniently – it has arrived in kitchens worldwide.

METHOD

1 Place the kefir grains in clean glass jar.

2 Add the milk, heated to blood temperature.

3 Cover with cloth fastened with elastic band.

4 Leave at room temperature for 12-24 hours, stirring two or three times during fermentation.

5 Strain now for drinking kefir. For cheese, leave to ferment for another 12-24 hours.

6 Pour the well-fermented kefir into a cloth-lined strainer positioned over a bowl.

7 Balance a wooden spoon over a container and suspend from it the kefir, wrapped in cloth, for 8-10 hours.

8 Remove the strained kefir cheese from the cloth and store in a glass jar in the fridge.

9 Eat as is, or add fresh chopped herbs or dried fruit or spices to taste.

TASTING NOTES

Kefir is thrillingly alive. Its seeds are, in fact, colonies of bacterial culture that feel and look like spongey cauliflower florets. Fed with warm milk, they become active; quickly the brew starts to fizz and exudes a deliciously yeasty smell. Traditional kefir was fermented in a bag of animal skin that was hung outside the house so that passers-by would swing it to keep the milk and seeds well mixed. In a modern household, a glass bottle or jar covered with cheesecloth is stirred or shaken by whoever enters the kitchen. After a few hours, kefir is ready to drink. Lightly effervescent, with the smoothness of drinking yoghurt, it's the perfect accompaniment to simple flatbread for breakfast on the road or a soothing after-dinner digestif in an urban deli– a cultured drink in any culture! ● *by Virginia Jealous*

JANE SWEENEY, JOANNAWNUK © GETTY IMAGES

ORIGINS

Bee pollen has a long history as a food supplement and natural medicine – ancient cultures from a number of parts of the world have made use of it, often along with honey. Hippocrates was a fan 2500 years ago, so what better vehicle for it than a traditional Greek porridge, made with barley.

SERVES 1

GREECE

BEE POLLEN PORRIDGE

When the great-great-granddaddy of Western medicine gives a food the thumbs up, you just know it's going to be good for you. Luckily it's delicious to eat as well!

YOU'LL NEED

¼ cup of barley flakes
1 cup of milk or water
a pinch of salt
sweetener if desired – honey
  or brown sugar, to taste
½ tsp cinnamon
1 tbs plain Greek yoghurt
1 tsp **bee pollen**

METHOD

1 Combine all ingredients except the bee pollen and yoghurt in a saucepan and bring to the boil

2 Cook on low heat for about 10 minutes, stirring every now and then till it becomes thick and creamy.

3 Serve in a bowl, add a little extra milk if you like, then top with the yoghurt and sprinkle with bee pollen.

TIP *A good porridge is one you've adjusted to your own tastes – find a blend of sweeteners, spices and fruit that works for your palate – but always remember the bee pollen.*

TASTING NOTES

Set the scene and take this recipe to winter (though a cool Bircher muesli could work well in summer) where the warming sustenance of the porridge is supercharged by the power of the pollen. A barley porridge has a nuttier taste than one made with oats. With a touch of raw sugar or honey and some thick Greek yoghurt, it's a hearty, satisfying blend of textures, temperatures and flavours. Then the magic ingredient: the floral, earthy, sweetness of the bee pollen. Bee pollen varies in taste, depending on the flowers that have contributed to the harvest, but you can rely on its nutty sweetness to carry you through a cold winter's morning. ● *by Ben Handicott*

SIVAN ASKAYO © LONELY PLANET, NATALIIKAEVSTI © GETTY IMAGES

ORIGINS

Hard-boiled eggs date back to antiquity, but tea eggs are a distinctly Asian twist on a classic dish. It's likely that the tea egg's distinctive flavouring and cooking method developed as a way to keep the dish palatable longer in the days prior to refrigeration. Tea, of course, is traditionally Chinese, though nowadays tea is but one of the dish's spicing agents, with star anise, soy sauce and other spices being the more dominant flavours.

TAIWAN AND CHINA

TEA EGGS

SERVES 6

**This tasty snack food is found throughout Taiwan.
A tea-egg crock pot is as ubiquitous in a Taiwanese convenience
store as a hot-dog roller grill in an American 7-11.**

YOU'LL NEED

6 large **eggs**
2 tbs loose black tea,
  or 2 teabags
¼ cup dark soy sauce
1–2 whole star anise

METHOD

1 Hard-boil the eggs. Remove from the heat and allow to cool for handling.

2 Tap the eggs all over with the back of a spoon so the shells crack (do not peel – the cracking allows the flavour to seep in).

3 Place the eggs in a pan, ideally one large enough for all six eggs to fit on the bottom. Cover with the tea, soy sauce and star anise, and enough water to cover the eggs fully.

4 Bring to the boil, then simmer on a low heat (a crock pot works nicely), with the pan uncovered, for 90 minutes, adding water as needed.

5 Your resulting tea eggs, when peeled, should have a nice marbled look, with the egg whites being tan with darker streaks of brown. The yolks should be dark yellow, with a greenish/grey tinge.

TASTING NOTES

Two things you can count on experiencing the moment the automatic doors slide open in any Taiwanese convenience store: a cheerful shout of *huanying* (welcome!) from behind the counter, and the distinctive soy-sauce and black-tea aroma of tea eggs wafting from the store's ready-to-eat section. The tea eggs will be in a crock pot (usually next to the steam tower containing warm buns, another Taiwanese convenience-store staple) ready to be placed into waiting plastic bags with tongs, or slipped into a pocket on a chilly day. Already cracked during the cooking process, the shells should fall away easily. You'll make short work of the snack, eating the tan egg white and creamy yellow yolk in a few tasty bites.
● *by Joshua Samuel Brown*

JOWENA CHUA © GETTY IMAGES, LOTTIE DAVIES © LONELY PLANET

SERVES 2

YOU'LL NEED

2 large **avocados**, ripe but
  not overly so (a day or two
  away from being suitable
  for guacamole should do)
4 small or medium **eggs**
salt, pepper and paprika, to
  taste
crisp-fried bacon bits,
  crumbled
croutons and/or crisp-fried
garlic, to serve (optional)

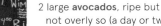

ORIGINS

Baked egg dishes are a brunch
classic, and omelettes –
especially in the American
Southwest, where this dish may
have originated – have long been
made using diced avocado as a
filling or served with a side order
of guacamole. At some point
we can only assume a clever
chef realised that removing the
avocado's pit left a hole large
enough to accommodate a small
egg and decided that combining
two of nature's more ovoid foods
would result in a tasty (and
rather photogenic) dish.

KRIS DAVIDSON © LONELY PLANET. BRENT HOFACKER © ALAMY

EGGS BAKED IN AVOCADO

Creamy, zesty, and more buttery than a dish without butter should be, eggs baked in avocado are guaranteed to impress superfood seekers of the culinary unique.

METHOD

1 Preheat the oven to 220°C (425°F).

2 Cut the unpeeled avocados in half, then remove the pits with a small spoon and enlarge the hole if necessary (depending upon the relative size of the avocados and the eggs).

3 Crack the eggs into a bowl, taking care not to break the yolks.

4 Arrange the avocado halves in a baking tray or ovenproof dish so the cut sides are facing up and are as level as possible.

5 Carefully place one egg yolk into each avocado half, then add enough egg white to each to completely fill the cavities. The best way to scoop up an egg yolk is to use an empty egg shell as a receptacle.

6 Season with salt, pepper and paprika to taste.

7 Carefully place the baking tray or ovenproof dish in the oven and bake for 12–15 minutes, depending on the desired consistency of the cooked eggs.

8 Remove the tray or dish from the oven and transfer the avocados to serving plates, allowing two halves per person.

9 Add bacon bits, crumbled croutons or fried garlic if desired.

TIP *Match the size of your eggs and avocados, using a spoon to make the hole left by the pit larger if necessary. And arrange the avocado halves snugly in a baking tray or so that the uncooked egg doesn't spill out.*

TASTING NOTES

The first thing you'll notice about this dish is its aesthetic prettiness. The sunshine-yellow yolk surrounded by a white ring floating inside the deep green oval of a halved avocado has a fun, almost Dr Seuss-like quality to it. The dish is equally pleasurable to eat, the avocado's creamy texture combining perfectly with the eggs to create something as easy to eat with a spoon as it is to spread over freshly toasted bread. As with any egg dish, the final texture depends on the cooking time, so your yolk can be anything from lightly poached to solid, depending on your preference. Diners looking to add crunch can sprinkle crispy bacon bits, fried garlic or croutons on the top, while those seeking a more Southwestern flavour will want to add a dash of hot sauce and perhaps some piquant salsa. ● *by Joshua Samuel Brown*

SARKA BABICKA © GETTY IMAGES

ORIGINS

Morocco, Libya and Tunisia all claim *shakshouka* as their own, but these assertions are hotly disputed in Israel, where *shak-shouka* is practically considered a national dish. The name is also up for debate: an evolution of *chakchouka*, the Berber word for 'ragout'; derived from *leshakshej* meaning 'to shake' in Hebrew; or adopted from *shak-shouka*, which is Arabic slang for 'all mixed up'.

YOU'LL NEED

1½ tbs **olive oil**

1 small onion, peeled and sliced

1 large **red (bell) pepper**, deseeded and thinly sliced

2 **garlic cloves**, peeled and thinly sliced

½ tsp ground cumin

½ tsp paprika

cayenne pepper, to taste

400g (14oz) canned whole **plum tomatoes** with juice, roughly chopped

salt and ground black pepper, to taste

4 **eggs**

coriander (cilantro), chopped to garnish

fresh bread, to serve (optional)

TASTING NOTES

The frying pan arrives at the table, still sizzling from the oven, and almost always with a word of warning from the waiter – 'Careful, it's hot'. A perfect *shakshouka's* egg yolks are still soft and bright yellow, just ready to be split and spilled into the rest of the ingredients. It's the deep flavours of the tomato sauce that are really the making of this dish, that warm smell of paprika, cayenne pepper and cumin spurring you on to soak up every last smear. Normally one order of *shakshouka* is considered big enough for two to share, but done right it's so moreish one person could easily demolish the lot. ● *by Helen Elfer*

ISRAEL AND NORTH AFRICA

SHAKSHOUKA

SERVES 2

Gorgeously rich and smoky, this breakfast of eggs, red pepper and tomato sauce gives you a warm glow in your belly and a superfood soul that will last the rest of the day.

METHOD

1 Preheat the oven to 190°C (375°F).

2 Heat the oil in a large ovenproof frying pan over a medium heat.

3 Add the onion and bell pepper.

4 Reduce the heat to low and cook the onion and pepper, stirring occasionally, for about 20 minutes, until soft.

5 Add the garlic and cook for a further 3–4 minutes, until softened.

6 Stir in the cumin, paprika and cayenne pepper and cook for 1 minute.

7 Pour the tomatoes into the frying pan.

8 Season the mixture with salt and pepper.

9 Simmer the mixture for about 10 minutes, until the sauce has thickened.

10 Using the back of a spoon, create four hollows in the sauce for the eggs to sit in.

11 Gently crack the eggs into the frying pan over the tomatoes.

12 Add more salt and pepper to taste.

13 Transfer the frying pan to the oven.

14 Bake for 7–10 minutes, until the eggs are set.

15 Sprinkle with coriander and serve immediately, with fresh bread if you like.

RICHARD I'ANSON © GETTY IMAGES

LUCIDPHOTO © GETTY IMAGES

ORIGINS

Chawan-mushi has been around for centuries, possibly dating as far back as the Heian period (794–1185) when court banquets were the rage among the aristocracy. This pale and silky steamed egg custard, which is filled with pieces of chicken, prawn, ginkgo nuts and lotus root and garnished with mitsuba leaf, is likely to have started life as a soup – it's one of only a few Japanese dishes to be eaten with a spoon.

YOU'LL NEED

For the dashi

5cm (2in) piece of **kombu** (dried seaweed)
1L (1.75 pints) water
1 cup *katsuobuoshi* (bonito flakes)

For the filling

80g (3oz) **chicken** breast, diced
1 tsp light soy sauce
1 tsp cooking sake
4 small raw prawns, peeled, deveined and blanched in hot water for about 30 seconds
4 water chestnuts or sliced bamboo shoots or sliced button mushrooms

For the custard

4 medium **eggs**
2½ cups **chicken stock** or dashi, at room temperature
1 tbs *mirin* (rice wine)
1 tbs light soy sauce
pinch of salt
small **parsley** or coriander leaves and/or lemon zest, for garnishing

TASTING NOTES

This is as light and delicate as egg dishes come. Creamy, slippery-smooth *chawan-mushi* is a delight to eat, with comforting mouthfuls of soft egg punctuated with morsels of meat and vegetables. The use of *dashi* or Japanese fish stock lends the dish its characteristic *umami* savouriness, while the fillings make for a tasty treasure hunt. At Japan's most prestigious restaurants, revered chefs elevate the humble dish to tantalising heights with the expert preparation of quivering custard and the use of the finest, seasonal ingredients such as the slightly bitter and unique-tasting ginkgo nut or the matsutake mushroom. ● *by Johanna Ashby*

JAPAN

CHAWAN-MUSHI

SERVES 4

Seemingly humble and delicate, yet at the same time intensely flavoured, Japan's ultimate egg dish is an intriguingly savoury and refreshing delight that will ease you into the day.

METHOD

1 To make the dashi, soak the kombu in the water in a small pan for at least 30 minutes.

2 Bring the water to the boil, removing the kombu just before it boils.

3 As soon as the water has boiled, add the *katsuobuoshi*, then turn off the heat.

4 Let the *katsuobuoshi* infuse for 1–2 minutes.

5 Strain the *dashi* through muslin or kitchen paper into a bowl and set aside.

6 To prepare the filling, marinate the chicken breast in the light soy sauce and sake for about 15 minutes.

7 Discard the marinade and set the chicken aside.

8 To make the custard, beat the eggs in a bowl.

9 Add the dashi, *mirin* (rice wine), soy sauce and salt.

10 Place a bamboo steamer over a pan of simmering water.

11 Divide the fillings evenly between four heatproof cups.

12 Strain the egg mixture into the cups, filling them to 1.5cm (⅔in) from the top.

13 Cover each cup with cling film or foil.

14 Place the cups in the steamer and cover with the lid.

15 Steam the custards for about 15 minutes, until the custard is set, ie slightly jiggling but not cracked or too firm.

16 Garnish with a parsley or coriander leaf and serve immediately, or leave to cool down if serving chilled.

A LONGER SPEECH © GETTY IMAGES

ORIGINS

Residue of the shallow-water seaweed was found in Japanese ceramics made in 3000 BC. So concentrated were the seaweed's levels of nutrients that the oldest law drafted in Japan stated that it be used as a tax, along with other seaweeds such as nori and arame. It quickly became a delicacy, being widely consumed in imperial court and shrines, while the surplus reached the masses at markets. Today, seaweed continues to be an essential part of Japan's diet.

SERVES 2

JAPAN

WAKAME SALAD

This sweet yet salty salad made of shallow-water wakame seaweed teamed with sesame and soy sauce is Japan's answer to a side of dark, life-giving greens. It's the perfect way to turn a sushi platter into a balanced meal.

YOU'LL NEED

50g (1oz) dried **wakame seaweed**
1 tbs **miso paste**
1 tbs tamari soy sauce
1 tbs *mirin*
1 tbs **sesame seeds**
1 tbs **sesame oil**
1 tsp lemon juice
1 red chilli, finely sliced
pinch of sea salt

METHOD

1 Rehydrate the wakame by placing it in a bowl of water

2 Combine the miso, soy sauce, *mirin*, sesame seeds, sesame oil, lemon juice, chilli and salt in a bowl, stirring with a whisk.

3 Drain the seaweed and place in a bowl.

4 Pour over the dressing and stir.

5 Add extra sesame seeds and chilli as desired before serving.

TASTING NOTES

With its heaped-up glistening dark-green tendrils flecked with sesame seeds, this sea vegetable salad exudes health and vitality. It has a satisfying chewy texture and a sweet-tart taste that is an instant palette refresher and great accompaniment to grilled fish and sushi. A popular side dish or appetizer at *izakayas* (Japanese pubs), use this tasty morsel to get your digestive juices flowing before tucking into the fish pick of the day. Sit at the bar and share with friends as you kick back in the early evening amid the hullabaloo of chatter: even if you're discussing the Tokyo sites you have visited rather than your hard day at work. ● *by Helen Brown*

OCSANADEN © GETTY IMAGES

ORIGINS

Although harvested by Aztecs in the 16th century and an everyday food of the Kanembu people of Chad, it was the health food craze of the 1980s that made spirulina popular in New Zealand, initially as a dietary supplement. By the noughties, long before kale was cool, spirulina smoothies were on cafe menus across the country as health-conscious customers relished the vivid-green pick-me-up. Bottles of the fruit juice now stand proud on supermarket shelves.

MAKES
2 LARGE
GLASSES

NEW ZEALAND

SPIRULINA SMOOTHIE

Green juices are so fashionable and the addition of spirulina
to a zingy blend of banana, kiwifruit, apple and orange gives
a vibrant emerald-green glass of goodness to pep up your day.

YOU'LL NEED

2 **apples,** cored
1 ripe **banana**, peeled
1 **kiwifruit**, peeled
1 seedless **orange**, peeled
2 tsp **spirulina** powder
1 cup water

METHOD

1 Place everything together in a blender.

2 Blend for about 1 minute, until smooth. The drink will be very
thick so add some more water if you prefer it more liquid.

3 Pour into a glass and slurp away.

TASTING NOTES

Drinking a spirulina smoothie is like snacking on a fruit bowl with an ocean breeze on your
face. The taste is one thing; smooth banana hints rise through tangy apple and orange while
tart kiwifruit zest up the taste buds and there's a faintly minerally after-taste. The texture is
another; thick and pulpy and just a little bit grainy. Then there's the look; it's eye-smackingly
green and, quite frankly, looks like it's been dredged up from the bottom of a pond.
Gulp it lolling in your boardies and jandals, watching surfers ride the
waves. Sip it as you rub elbows with a sleeve-tattooed dude in an inner-city joint. And
remember, when it comes to juice, green is the new orange. ● *by Tracy Whitmey*

GRANT ROONEY | PREMIUM, ELENA SHASHKINA © ALAMY, MACK READ © LONELY PLANET

YOU'LL NEED

16 whole prawns
1 white onion, peeled and
 finely chopped
100g (3.5oz) unsalted butter,
 diced
400g (14oz) carnarolli rice
 (arborio rice is a suitable
 replacement)
1½ tsp **plankton** powder
1 cup white wine
2L (4 pints) fish stock
juice of 1 lemon

ORIGINS

These infinitesimally small
creatures first appeared on
the radar of London's foodies
in 2013, thanks to Spanish chef
Ángel León, who figured out how
to how to harness phytoplankton
flavours at his Michelin-starred
Aponiente restaurant in Cádiz.
Along with fellow chef Nuno
Mendes, he then created a special menu at the latter's Michelin-starred restaurant Viajante
in London (now closed). Another
fine-dining establishment in
London currently experimenting
with plankton is the Basque
restaurant Ametsa.

NUMB © ALAMY

LONDON, ENGLAND

PLANKTON RISOTTO

Innovative chefs have discovered a microscopic ingredient that raises the classic prawn risotto to new culinary heights and has seafood lovers enraptured: pungent-smelling, silky-textured plankton.

METHOD

1 Clean and remove the heads, then roughly chop the prawns, saving the juice from their heads.

2 Heat 1 tablespoon of butter in a wide-bottomed pan and saute the onion until it becomes soft and translucent.

3 Add the rice, plankton powder and prawn-head juice, stirring for 3 minutes on medium heat.

4 Add the white wine and cook at a high heat until the wine has been absorbed.

5 Turn down the heat and add a ladleful of fish stock, stirring until it has been absorbed. Continue this process of adding stock and stirring until the rice is al dente, which should take 15-20 minutes (you may not need to use all the stock).

6 Add the raw prawns to the risotto and cook for 2-3 minutes until they are done.

7 Add the diced butter and lemon juice to the risotto, stirring until the former has melted and the mixture has acquired a creamy texture.

TASTING NOTES

There is something immensely satisfying about seafood risotto: the creaminess of the sauce, the al dente texture of the rice, the salty taste and firmness of prawn flesh, the marine flavours, imparted by the fish stock and enhanced by prawn head juices. Imagine yourself in a refined setting: white linen, subdued lighting, the whisper of cloth as your waiter silently appears at your side. Then your risotto is placed in front of you, its surface a deep swamp green, its scent evoking the ocean whence the plankton came. Its velvety, seductive texture caresses your tongue and the beach-in-your-mouth flavour lingers on your palate after each mouthful. ● *by Anna Kaminski*

MULTI-BITS, MAREMAGNUM © GETTY IMAGES

ORIGINS

Kimchi's history began in the 16th century when the Japanese brought chilli peppers to the Korean peninsula. Though initially regarded with suspicion, they became mainstream due to food shortages. By the mid-18th century, spicy kimchi made with cucumbers, eggplant and radish was commonplace. Today's iconic dish with Napa cabbage, probably first appeared on dining tables around the 1900s.

YOU'LL NEED

1 large head of Napa (also known as Chinese or celery) **cabbage**

3 tbs sea salt or non-iodized salt

5–8 spring onions (scallions), chopped into 2cm (1in) pieces

1 small yellow onion, sliced

4–6 **garlic cloves**, crushed

4 tbs **ginger root**, crushed

2 tbs sugar (white or brown)

1 tbs *nuoc mam* (fish sauce)

4–6 tbs red chilli flakes

TASTING NOTES

To appreciate *kimchi's* culinary versatility, head to a Korean barbecue restaurant. Rustic eateries, the ones with gravel floors and stainless steel tables, are fun budget choices frequented by boisterous patrons eager to pour another round of drinks. On the grill, long strips of pork belly crackle and sizzle over red-hot charcoal. When gentle plumes of smoke begin to rise, it is time to grill *kimchi*. A few minutes of moderate heat yields a zesty, brilliant orange condiment. Lettuce wraps with a layer of fresh sesame leaf, pork, and garlic topped off with *kimchi* are common. Fold it up in your hand and eat with gusto. Then, pour a round to celebrate an incredible Korean dinner. ● *by Rob Whyte*

SERVES 8 AS
A SIDE DISH

KIMCHI

A meal in Korea just isn't complete without this salty, pungent and, at times, overpowering fermented Chinese (also known as Napa or celery) cabbage seasoned with red chilli flakes, garlic and ginger.

METHOD

1 Remove wilted cabbage leaves and wash the outside of the cabbage under running water.

2 Cut the cabbage lengthwise into four quarters, then place it in a colander and rinse thoroughly, squeezing the pieces to remove excess water.

3 Place the cabbage on a chopping board and cut into 2cm (1in) squares, then put the cut cabbage into a large bowl.

4 Sprinkle salt on the cabbage, and toss with your hands to distribute the salt evenly.

5 Add enough water to cover the cabbage in the bowl and then cover with a plate and let stand for two hours.

6 Place the cabbage in a colander and drain the brine. Remove it to a bowl and rinse under cold water three times. Return the cabbage to the colander and let drain it for 15 minutes.

7 Combine the spring onions, onion, garlic, ginger, sugar and fish sauce in a bowl, and add the red chilli flakes to make it into a spicy paste; adjust according to taste.

8 Transfer the cabbage from the colander to a large bowl. Add the spicy paste to the cabbage, and mix well with your hands (wearing plastic gloves is recommended). Be sure all cabbage is coated with the spicy paste.

9 Place the cabbage in sterilised canning jars or plastic containers and close with tight-fitting lids, then let sit for 1–2 days at room temperature.

10 Store in the fridge up to 1 month after opening.

ORIGINS

It's easy to trace the origins of yogi tea, as the drink inspired a million-dollar company, but the brew was first created by a Punjabi Sikh guru called Yogi Bhajan, who traced a trail of hippie love to America, introducing the West to *kundalini* yoga in the process. In fact, his refreshing blend of cinnamon, cardamom, ginger, cloves and black pepper draws on ancient ayurvedic infusions, prepared in India since time immemorial.

SERVES 4

INDIA

YOGI TEA

Nothing sets you up for a morning of yoga quite like yogi tea, an inspired combination of tea leaves, cardamom, cinnamon, pepper, cloves and ginger, like Indian *chai* on overdrive.

YOU'LL NEED

4 cups water
2.5cm (1in) piece **ginger root**, peeled
12 green **cardamom pods**
12 whole black peppercorns
12 whole cloves
2.5cm (1in) piece of cinnamon stick
2 tsp black tea leaves
2 cups milk
honey, to taste

TIP *For a vegan version, use soy, almond or coconut milk, and omit the honey.*

METHOD

1 Bring the water to the boil in a small pan.

2 Cut the ginger into thick slices.

3 Crack the cardamom pods with the flat side of a knife.

4 Add all the spices to the boiling water and cover and boil for 15 minutes.

5 Add the tea leaves and allow to steep for a few minutes, then add the milk and return to the boil.

6 As soon as the liquid starts to boil, remove from the heat and strain into four cups.

7 Sweeten with honey to taste, and feel refreshed!

TASTING NOTES

You're a few generations too late to join the hippies who followed Yogi Bhajan into the summer of love, though his 3HO Foundation is still going strong, but a surfside yoga class on a Goan beach isn't a bad place to sample your first cup of yogi tea. There's no point being refreshed if you aren't tired first, so allow a challenging hour of twisting and contorting before sampling this revitalising brew. Kick back under a tropical palm and sip slowly to appreciate the varied spicy overtones. Cinnamon and ginger come in atmospheric waves, mingling with the powerful tang of cloves, cardamom and pepper. It's a mix that wakens the senses and clears the sinuses; it's instantly refreshing and strangely calming – another health benefit in the hectic subcontinent! ● *by Joe Bindloss*

PHOTOCUISINE RM © ALAMY, AMAR GROVER © GETTY IMAGES, MATT MUNRO © LONELY PLANET

MATT MUNRO © LONELY PLANET

ANDREW MONTGOMERY © LONELY PLANET

AUTHORS

NATASHA CORRETT is a British chef, health-food writer and the founder of Honestly Healthy. She first started developing a real taste for flavours as a 16-year-old when spending much of her summer holidays in the kitchen of one of her father's French restaurants. Her first book, *Honestly Healthy: Eat with your body in mind*, the alkaline way, was published in 2013 and became a bestseller. Her fifth (and latest) title, *Honestly Healthy in a hurry: The busy food-lover's cookbook* was published by Hodder & Stoughton in April 2016.

Kate Armstrong Food connoisseur and lover of all things sweet. Capable chef. Global taste buds. Stomach of steel. Nothing – except oysters – is off her menu.

Johanna Ashby Food and travel freelance writer and specialist author for Lonely Planet, keen on everything epicurean from street food to fine dining and everything in between. www.thehappydiner.co.uk.

Joe Bindloss Former food critic for Time Out's restaurant guides, specialising in food from Southeast Asia, China, Korea and the Indian subcontinent, and current Lonely Planet Destination Editor.

Tom Parker Bowles An award-winning food writer and critic, Tom has published five cookbooks, the latest – *Let's Eat Meat* – was published in 2015 by Pavilion.

Celeste Brash Contributor to *The World as a Kitchen*, writer of food sections for Lonely Planet guidebooks and www.lonelyplanet.com and erstwhile professional cook.

Helen Brown Former *Sunday Times Style* beauty editor Helen Brown is passionate about imparting healthy lifestyle advice, from diet to relaxation and exercise, through her work as a well-being journalist.

Joshua Samuel Brown When not on the road in Taiwan, Singapore or Belize, Joshua is eating food from trucks in Portland, Oregon. He writes about travel and food for Lonely Planet.

Austin Bush Writer of Thai food blog www.austinbushphotography.com, food writer for guidebooks, magazines including *Saveur*, *Travel + Leisure Southeast Asia*, *Chile Pepper*, and *DestinAsian*.

Sarah P Gilbert is a Sydney-based writer, journalist and television producer. An avid baker and traveller, she has broken bread in at least 30 countries.

Ben Handicott Once published travel pictorial and reference books for a living, now dreams about, writes about and sometimes even does, travel. Eats and drinks too.

Anita Isalska Travel editor, freelance writer and gluten-free gourmand. Anita blogs about her life in food at www.madamefreefrom.blogspot.co.uk.

Virginia Jealous Having travelled and eaten her way around the world for Lonely Planet since 1999, she remains addicted to Balinese black rice pudding.

Bailey Johnson Lonely Planet Destination Editor raised on cheesy, buttery Southern American fare who possesses a fierce love for Latin American cuisine.

Anna Kaminski When not on the road in Latin America or Southeast Asia, Anna seeks out the strangest regional specialities in her native UK. Seafood and haggis are her weaknesses.

Adam Karlin A US-based Lonely Planet author who loves to eat, wander and combine the two whenever possible.

Patrick Kinsella Pat has followed his stomach all over the globe, seeking superfoods and flavoursome fuel for footpacking adventures, but says Australia's brilliant bush tucker takes the (wattleseed) biscuit.

Rebecca Law Becky's food travels don't end at home – she continues to work her way around the globe via the obscure international ingredients available at her local grocery in London. Each time she leaves with a bag of stories waiting to be told.

Catherine Le Nevez Lonely Planet writer primarily based (wanderlust aside) in foodie mecca Paris; Doctor of Creative Arts in Writing; Bloody Mary devotee.

Daniel McCrohan Originally from the UK, Daniel has been eating and drinking his way through China for more than a decade. Follow his temptingly tasty travels at www.danielmccrohan.com.

Karyn Noble Superfoodie Karyn wrote all the chapter introductions for this book, loving every second of channelling her inner nutritionist. When not obsessing over food, she's a senior editor in Lonely Planet's London office and an award-winning freelance writer. Her thanks go to Tom Parker Bowles for his cameo in the Fish & Meat chapter. She tweets (usually food photos) at @MsKarynNoble.

Etain O'Carroll Author of over 20 Lonely Planet guidebooks, Etain loves to bake and writes here about favourite dishes from a childhood in the west of Ireland.

Katie O'Connell A Melbourne-based Lonely Planet editor and writer, keen home cook, cheese and beer connoisseur, and regular sampler of Melbourne's restaurant scene.

Matt Phillips As Matt is constantly looking for superfoods to fuel his energetic endeavours, whether summiting the world's largest dunes in Namibia, jogging up to Monserrate in Bogotá or running stairs at Lonely Planet's London office, he was the obvious choice to oversee *The World's Best Superfoods* title – he managed to pen a few of his favourite recipes too. When not exercising, eating, travelling or working within Lonely Planet's Trade & Reference department, he is the Destination Editor for sub-Saharan Africa. He tweets and instagrams his adventures at @Go2MattPhillips.

Sarah Reid Travel journalist, former Lonely Planet Destination Editor and eternal globetrotter, Sarah has sampled the classic foodie delights of more than 70 countries.

Simon Richmond Writer, photographer and enthusiastic epicurean, Simon has gleefully eaten his way around the world enjoying everything from sea urchin in Japan and seaweed lasagne in Cape Town to tapenade on the Côte d'Azur.

Daniel Robinson Author of food reviews – and Lonely Planet guides – of culinary hot spots such as Israel, Tunisia, Cambodia, Borneo, France and Germany.

Phillip Tang Anywhere with wafts of coriander and charcoal prawns has already seduced Phillip. He writes for Lonely Planet on China, Japan, Korea, Mexico, Peru and Canada. More eats: www.philliptang.co.uk.

Rebecca Warren After purchasing her first cookbook at the age of eight, a career as a food editor was inevitable. Born in the American South and enchanted by the British Isles, Rebecca loves the way regional food reveals the essence of a place.

Luke Waterson Luke writes about the culinary culture of different destinations for publications from Lonely Planet to the *Telegraph*, and on everything from reindeer in Finland to rum in Cuba. www.lukeandhiswords.com/culinary-travel/

Tracy Whitmey A self-confessed foodie and keen cook, Tracy is a Lonely Planet editor and freelance writer. She's usually found hanging around food markets asking 'What is it?' and 'How do you cook it?'.

Rob Whyte A resident of South Korea for 15 years, Rob has tried most of the local specialties including baby octopus, though grilled pork with kimchi remains his all-time favourite Korean food.

INDEX

BY LOCATION

MARK READ © LONELY PLANET

JUSTIN FOULKES © LONELY PLANET

The World's Best Superfoods

March 2017
Published by Lonely Planet Global Limited
CRN 554153

www.lonelyplanet.com

10 9 8 7 6 5 4 3 2 1

Printed in China
ISBN 978 1 78657 402 2
© Lonely Planet 2017
© photographers as indicated 2017

Managing Director, Publishing Piers Pickard
Associate Publisher Robin Barton
Commissioning Editor Matt Phillips
Art Director Daniel Di Paolo
Layout Designer Hayley Warnham
Content Researcher Christina Webb
Photography Researcher Ceri James
Cover Illustration David Doran
Editor Jeanette Wall
Sub-Editor Lucy Doncaster
Pre-Press Production Nigel Longuet
Print Production Larissa Frost

Written by Kate Armstrong, Johanna Ashby, Joe Bindloss, Tom Parker Bowles, Celeste Brash, Helen Brown, Joshua Samuel Brown, Austin Bush, Natasha Corrett, Sarah P Gilbert, Ben Handicott, Anita Isalska, Virginia Jealous, Bailey Johnson, Anna Kaminski, Adam Karlin, Patrick Kinsella, Rebecca Law, Catherine Le Nevez, Daniel McCrohan, Karyn Noble, Etain O'Carroll, Katie O'Connell, Matt Phillips, Sarah Reid, Simon Richmond, Daniel Robinson, Phillip Tang, Rebecca Warren, Luke Waterson, Tracy Whitmey, Rob Whyte

With thanks to Jessica Cole, Flora MacQueen, Claire Naylor, Karyn Noble.

All rights reserved. No part of this publication may be reproduced, stored in a retrieval system or transmitted in any form by any means, electronic, mechanical, photocopying, recording or otherwise except brief extracts for the purpose of review, without the written permission of the publisher. Lonely Planet and the Lonely Planet logo are trademarks of Lonely Planet and are registered in the US patent and Trademark Office and in other countries.

Lonely Planet Offices
AUSTRALIA
The Malt Store, Level 3, 551 Swanston St, Carlton, Victoria 3053 T: 03 8379 8000

IRELAND
Unit E, Digital Court, The Digital Hub, Rainsford St, Dublin 8

USA
124 Linden St, Oakland, CA 94607 T: 510 250 6400

UK
240 Blackfriars Rd, London SE1 8NW T: 020 3771 5100

STAY IN TOUCH
lonelyplanet.com/contact

Although the authors and Lonely Planet have taken all reasonable care in preparing this book, we make no warranty about the accuracy or completeness of its content and, to the maximum extent permitted, disclaim all liability from its use.

Paper in this book is certified against the Forest Stewardship Council™ standards. FSC™ promotes environmentally responsible, socially beneficial and economically viable management of the world's forests.